GOD
JUST SHOWED
UP

To Margie,

may God bless you this
in your ministry and this
new journey that God has
prepared for you,

Lyssette
3/23/07

The Negro National Anthem

Lift every voice and sing
Till earth and heaven ring,
Ring with the harmonies of Liberty;
Let our rejoicing rise
High as the listening skies,
Let it resound loud as the rolling sea.
Sing a song full of the faith that the dark past has taught us,
Sing a song full of the hope that the present has brought us,
Facing the rising sun of our new day begun
Let us march on till victory is won.

So begins the Black National Anthem, by James Weldon Johnson in 1900. Lift Every Voice is the name of the joint imprint of The Institute for Black Family Development and Moody Press, a division of the Moody Bible Institute.

Our vision is to advance the cause of Christ through publishing African-American Christians who educate, edify, and disciple Christians in the church community through quality books written for African-Americans.

The Institute for Black Family Development is a national Christian organization. It offers degreed and nondegreed training nationally and internationally to established and emerging leaders from churches and Christian organizations. To learn more about The Institute for Black Family Development write us at:

The Institute for Black Family Development
15151 Faust
Detroit, Michigan 48223

Moody Press, a ministry of Moody Bible Institute,
is designed for education, evangelization, and edification.
If we may assist you in knowing more about Christ
and the Christian life, please write us without obligation:

Moody Press
c/o Moody Literature Ministries
820 N. LaSalle Blvd.
Chicago, Illinois 60610.

GOD
JUST SHOWED
UP

Stories of Hope in Everyday Experiences

Linda Watkins

For my Heavenly Father,
to You be the Glory
and
my parents, William and Sylvia Watkins,
for your love, faith and example

Library of Congress Cataloging-in-Publication Data

God just showed up : stories of hope in everyday experiences / Linda Watkins,
    general editor.
        p. cm.
    ISBN 0-8024-6591-9
        1. Christian biography—United States. 2. African Americans—Religious life.
    I. Watkins, Linda, 1962–

BR1700.3 .G63 2001
277.3'082'092396073—dc21
[B]

2001038170

3 5 7 9 10 8 6 4

Printed in the United States of America

CONTENTS

ACKNOWLEDGMENTS

[Jesus] said to his disciples, "A large crop is in the fields, but there are only a few workers. Ask the Lord in charge of the harvest to send out workers to bring it in."

MATTHEW 9:37–38 (AJE)

Four years ago, the Lord planted a seed in my heart. It was the concept for the book you are reading. Over the years, God watered the seed and sent forth people to help it grow. I thank each person who heard the call and answered with love and ready hands.

A dedicated group of sisters and brothers prayed for the successful completion of this book for three whole years! They are: Reverend Cynthia Kenderson, Barbara Russell, Chris Eisom, Lois Broadus, Debbie Taylor, Reverend Phyllis James, Reverend Joan Prentice, Elizabeth Tillman, Helen Clark, Joyce Giddens, Reverend Leslie Regan, Elder Enos C. Scott, and Dr. Harrison Mensah. Thanks so much for your prayers and incredible faithfulness! You have truly been your sister's keeper.

Talented writers and Christian educators helped gather, write, and edit stories for the book. They are: Michele Drayton, Salatheia Bryant-Honors, Susan Wright, Carmen Lee, Linda T. Richardson,

Sharon Flake, Sonya Toler, Sheldon Ingram, Virginia Cunningham, Avis Marcus, Dr. Alice Brown Collins, and Reverend Mary Louise Buckley. Thanks for caring about the quality of the stories in this book. Thanks for sharing your writing and editing gifts to help reach the harvest.

Technology made our job easier. E-mail and faxes saved a lot of time. But I'm even more thankful for the people God sent with financial gifts to cover project expenses. They are: Hilary Borneo, the Curtis Martin Job Foundation, William and Sylvia Watkins, Cheryl and Roland Snead, Barbara Russell, Oliver Byrd, Elaine Atkinson, Joyce and Robert Giddens, Diane Hunt, René Payne, Reverend Phyllis James, Jeffrey Richardson, Dr. Helen Faison, Monumental Missions Ministries, Dolores Williams, Larry Pickett, Charles Reaves, and Michele Drayton. May God return to you tenfold what you sowed into this book! Thanks for being generous givers and sharing your wealth in the spirit of Ujamaa.

Others also made invaluable contributions. J. Richardson Consultants loaned me a computer and printer for the first year of the project. Donna W. Adkins provided swift and accurate transcription services. René Payne Design blessed the project with creative-design support. Morningside Church of God in Christ and Faith Restoration Ministries opened their doors for several of our prayer meetings. I thank all of you for seeing the vision and responding to our needs in such incredibly helpful ways.

Next, I would like to express deep gratitude to my spiritual mentors and teachers. They are Elder Raymond Clark, Mother Willa M. Johnson, Deacon Vernon Franklin, Reverend Phyllis James, Evangelist Lois Broadus, Bishop Joseph L. Garlington, Pastor Barbara Garlington, and Pastor Leroy Joseph. Thanks for opening up the Scriptures to me. There's no greater gift in the world! Thank you, sisters and brothers of the Willa M. Johnson School of Bible and Ministry for your prayers and support over the years.

Throughout this project and before, my family has been a tremendous blessing in my life. Dad and Mom, Cheryl and René, all of my ancestors without whom I would not exist, I love, thank, and cherish you.

Last but not least are special friends who were there for me during this project. Jeffrey, thanks for your love, kindness, and support. Cynthia, Andrea, Rev. Patricia, Michele, Debbie, Erica and Kim, thanks for being my sistuhs!

Through God, everyone named above, Greg Thornton, Cynthia Ballenger, Pamela J. Pugh, and Dave DeWit of Moody Press, the Lift Every Voice Editorial Review Board and The Institute for Black Family Development, the seed became a book. May *God Just Showed Up* speak, first and foremost, to every precious soul that is part of the harvest.

Linda Watkins
January 2001

CONTRIBUTING WRITERS

Salatheia Bryant-Honors is a reporter for the *Houston Chronicle*. She has been a reporter for thirteen years. Bryant-Honors is also a member of Evangelist Chapel A.M.E. Church in Houston. She was called into the preaching ministry in January 1999 and is expected to be ordained as an itinerant deacon by the A.M.E. church. She is married to Reverend Reginald Honors. Bryant-Honors graduated from Auburn University with a degree in journalism.

Michele Drayton has worked professionally as a reporter since 1988 at metropolitan newspapers in New Jersey, Connecticut, and Florida. She also has worked for an Internet company. Drayton completed freelance work overseas for a Washington, D.C.–based magazine. She lives in Tampa, Florida, where she attends Bible Based Fellowship Church of Temple Terrace.

Sheldon Ingram is a reporter for WTAE-TV in Pittsburgh. His journalism career began in 1987 at CNN in Atlanta where he was an intern reporter. From there, he served as a reporter and news anchor for WRCB-TV in Chattanooga. He held the same position at WVEC-TV in Norfolk, Virginia, before starting at WTAE in 1992. Ingram is a member of Covenant Church of Pittsburgh. His home is Atlantic City, New Jersey. He is a graduate of Morris Brown College in Atlanta.

Sharon L. Narcisse is the founder and president of In Him Ministries, a consulting agency that provides self-awareness workshops and seminars for women. The organization's mission is to help at-risk women realize that they have the power, knowledge, gifts, and ability to develop into strong women through the power of God. Narcisse lives in Somerset, Pennsylvania, with her three children.

Linda T. Richardson is a parent liaison for the Baltimore County Public Schools' Office of Community and Parent Relations. She is a writer whose articles have been published in school and Parent Teacher Association newsletters. Her goal is to publish more of her writing and to open a business through which young people can learn how to become entrepreneurs. Richardson is a member of New Psalmist Baptist Church in Baltimore. She is the mother of two children and resides in the Baltimore area with her husband.

Linda Watkins is a professional writer and a consultant to non-profit organizations. She began her writing career in 1984 as a staff reporter for the *Wall Street Journal*. She is a poet and playwright whose African-American history plays have been performed for young people and adults in Pennsylvania. In 1997, Ms. Watkins was called into the ministry of writing. *God Just Showed Up* is her first nonfiction book. She is a member of Covenant Church of Pittsburgh, a student of Moody Bible Institute's External Studies Program, and a graduate of Brown and Yale universities.

Susan Kimmel Wright is the author of Herald Press's *Dead-End Road* Christian mystery series for young readers, as well as many devotionals and articles in Christian and secular magazines, newspapers, and anthologies. She is an instructor for The Institute of Children's Literature. Wright is married and the mother of three teenagers.

INTRODUCTION

God Almighty is a personal God who is calling each of us to count on Him. He may show up at our sick bed or in the midst of a life-threatening accident. He may speak to us in a dream or right before a critical decision. Sometimes God sends angels to deliver a personal message or leads us to a Bible verse that heals our souls.

God Just Showed Up, Stories of Hope in Everyday Experiences is a collection of uplifting stories about nineteen African-Americans who discovered firsthand that God is the source of hope, peace, healing, and direction for our lives. Representing Black Americans from various walks of life—from a former crack addict to a world-renowned surgeon—they share true stories of a God who delivers His people from violence, drug addiction, illness, wounds of racism, and other life challenges.

The stories in this book convey a central message: 1) God is REAL and loves us all, regardless of our economic status, age, or spiritual condition, 2) God CAN DO ANYTHING from healing and providing for us to protecting and comforting us, and 3) God WANTS A PERSONAL RELATIONSHIP with all of His children. Our first step is to seek Him.

African-Americans have always had a special relationship with God. Our rich spiritual legacy dates all the way back to Adam.

In recent years, scholars have revealed the African presence in the Bible, from the Garden of Eden in ancient Northeast Africa to the Afro-Asiatic roots of Jesus Christ.

Perhaps one of the greatest tragedies of the late twentieth century was the large number of African-Americans who lost touch with God. Some stopped seeking Him. Others never knew Him. He is the same God who helped our ancestors survive the treacherous journey to America on slave ships. He is the God who brought our people out of slavery and marched beside us during the Civil Rights Movement. He is the same God who watches out for African-Americans today despite how far we, as a people, have strayed. Indeed, many challenges plaguing our communities today may relate as much to a spiritual void as to poverty and institutional racism. Regardless, the Lord continues to reach out to us.

For thousands of years God has longed for all of us to encounter Him. His plan from the start was to have a personal relationship with us, beginning with Adam and Eve in the Garden of Eden. His desire was never to be a distant God but rather a Father whose voice we would know and follow. When Adam and Eve sinned in the Garden, humankind became separated from God and the peace, love, and joy that come from walking with Him. The journey of life is a journey back to our Father. As we seek and follow God, He reveals more of Himself in and through our lives.

The stories in this book describe several aspects of God's huge personality. He is the God of hope, the God who makes a way out of no way, the God who heals, the God who guides our path, the God of second chances, the God who sticks closer than a brother, and so much more. God is all-powerful and knowing. He is a God of judgment but also mercy and love. King David, the writer of the one hundred and forty-fifth Psalm, says:

Great is the Lord, and greatly to be praised;
And His greatness is unsearchable.
One generation shall praise Your works to
another,
And shall declare Your mighty acts.
I will meditate on the glorious splendor of
Your majesty,
And on Your wondrous works.
Men [and women] shall speak of the might
of Your awesome acts,
And I will declare Your greatness.

PSALM 145:3–6 (NKJV)

The stories in *God Just Showed Up* seek to do that, to reveal just how much God is still in the blessing business. As you read these accounts of how God reaches out to touch the souls of Black folk today, let the Lord speak to your heart. Find yourself in the stories in this book. If you don't know God, He says, "Come. Welcome Me into your life." If you know about Him but really want to *know* Him, God says, "Seek Me and you will find Me." If you knew Him way back when but want to know Him again, it's not too late. The Lord says, "Return to Me."

At the dawn of this new millennium, God is calling us back to Him. As we, God's people, return to the Lord, as we humble ourselves and seek Him again, our lives, families, and communities will be enriched and restored.

1
THE GOD OF HOPE

Hope is a feeling that lives deep within. It's an anchor in times of trouble. It's the belief that something good is going to happen despite how bad things look. People with hope can rise above their challenges or persevere through them because they know a greater force is on their side.

For thousands of years, God has given hope to Black people and revealed Himself as the source of hope in our lives. Without hope, more enslaved Africans—horrified by the thought of a life in bondage—would have committed suicide on the treacherous Middle Passage from Africa to America. Without hope, thousands of civil rights marchers in the 1960s would not have put their lives on the line to win basic rights we enjoy today.

The stories in this chapter show how God continues to reveal Himself to those who put their hope in Him.

I look to the hills! Where will I find help?
It will come from the Lord, who created the
heavens and the earth.

PSALM 121:1–2 (AJE)

A REASON TO LIVE

Curtis Martin

Written by Linda Watkins

A lot of people know me as a running back for the New York Jets football team. They see my fame and fortune and think I always had it going on. But when I was growing up, I didn't expect to live past the age of twenty-one. Any day, any second, I thought I'd be dead because violence was part of my life. It was like I was on a life-support system and the monitor line was almost flat. The only reason I'm alive today is God.

By the time I reached the age of twenty, I was afraid to go to sleep at night because I kept on having this dream. There would always be a guy in the dream but I could see only half of his arm; in his hand was a gun pointed at me. I'd be standing against a brick wall with the sun shining down on me, and I'd be looking up at the sky instead of at the gun. As soon as the guy started to pull the trigger, I'd hear a voice: "Curt, duck your head."

As long as I listened to the voice, the bullet would miss me and hit my shadow on the wall. Night after night I had that dream, and it haunted me. I'd rather have been in an all-out war.

From the time I was a little kid, I was in survival mode. It started when I was in kindergarten and had to come home from school and stay in the house all alone. My mom was working three jobs just to keep food on our table. She'd make me stay inside because she feared something would happen to me if I went out. My mom couldn't afford a baby-sitter so I'd sit by the window watching other kids play. I was scared to death to move anywhere else in the house.

When I turned nine, my grandmother's murder reminded me I lived in a violent world. My mother and a maintenance man found my grandmother in her apartment lying in a bloody bed. A knife was stuck in her chest, through her heart, out her back, and her eyes were wide open. In the bedroom, blood was everywhere; in the kitchen, string beans were scattered. Grandma must have been cooking when the robber came for her money.

Growing up poor in the inner city makes you grow up fast. I started going to over-twenty-one clubs when I was fourteen years old. Back then, I drank liquor and messed around with women twice my age. I was living a life on the edge of a cliff and was almost killed many times. I'll never forget when I was in a high-speed car chase one Memorial Day in high school. I had a rental car. Me and my friend Tony pulled up to a red light when this big Mercedes Benz pulled up beside us.

"Which one of you guys' name is Tony?" the driver asked.[1]

"Hey, cuz, ain't nobody's name Tony, man. What's your name?" I answered.

The guy was all decked out in gold and diamonds. He snickered as he rolled up his window. Then he rolled his window back down. "You sure none of you guys' name is Tony?"

"Look, man, I told you ain't nobody's name is Tony." But my friend started panicking beside me.

"Hey, man, I swear to God my name ain't Tony! I swear to God! My name is Scotty." Right there he gave it away, and the guy in the Benz started laughing.

I was thinking he was gonna shoot us through the window, but instead he tried to ram our car off the road several minutes later. Both our cars were flying up a curving road in the rain. I was going maybe ninety miles per hour, and he was doing about the same. By some stroke of luck, every time he tried to hit us, I'd swerve, and he'd missed our car. My heart was pumping so fast, particularly when we crossed this one intersection. The guy in the Benz drove his car right in front of us to try to wipe us out. But anticipating his move, I hit my brakes. When our car finally stopped spinning, his headlights were in our faces.

Now back then because I always feared for my life, I'd practice different little things. One of them was driving backwards, and I'd gotten pretty good at it. So in this situation I quickly threw my car into reverse. We continued the high-speed chase, but now I was driving backwards! The speedometer read eighty-nine miles per hour as we flew up the wet, winding road.

Suddenly, my arm jerked, and I lost control of the wheel. My car spun 180 degrees, but amazingly it lined up perfectly in the lane I was in. It was like something out of a movie, but all this was really happening. I threw the car into drive with the Benz right on our tail.

Eventually I knew there was no way to shake the driver of the Benz, so when the chance came, we stopped, jumped out, and started flying on foot. At one point, I hid in a ditch between two houses. When I jumped down I landed on a rusty pipe that ripped through the side of my buttock. Blood was streaming down my leg, but I still managed to run about half a mile to a friend's house. During the drive to a hospital I realized that I'd been protected. The good news was, Tony made it out, too.

There were so many times when I made it through life-threatening situations that a lot of my friends used to think I was psychic. We'd be hanging out someplace, and all of a sudden I'd say, "Hey, let's leave. Let's leave." When they asked me why, I'd tell them, "I just got a bad feeling." As soon as we'd leave, we'd start hearing gunshots, and that happened lots of times.

Like I said, I was protected, but that didn't make me worry less. My nerves were so bad at seventeen, I used to break out in rashes all over my body. My main goal in life was to survive, even though I felt like I had no reason to live. There was no purpose or meaning to my life. Maybe that's why I lived like I was gonna die tomorrow.

My mother is the person I credit for getting me into football. Every time I walked out of the house, she'd have these big crocodile tears in her eyes. She knew I was heading for trouble somewhere in the streets, so her eyes would say what her mouth couldn't: "I really hope you come back today."

One day my mother said, "Curt, I want you to do something after school to occupy your time. Play soccer, join the glee club, play an instrument, *whatever.*"

So I started playing football during my senior year in high school. I never expected to break all kinds of records the first season I played. I didn't even like the game that much, but I had a phenomenal year. Schools across the country were calling me, offering full college scholarships to Penn State, Notre Dame, Georgia Tech, Miami, and other places. I figured I'd better go to college and play ball or I'd look really dumb. I chose the University of Pittsburgh because it was close to home. Just in case college didn't work out, I could still hang out with my partners.

A year later I was playing college ball, but nothing else in my life had changed. I just had to disguise my lifestyle. Teachers and coaches may have thought I was one of the nicest guys in the world, but people who really knew me saw me as a bad guy. I was deceitful, had a violent side, and my heart was real hard. Other football players may have been dreaming about a bright future in the NFL, but I was still having nightmares of the guy with the gun. Despite my success in football, I didn't plan ahead because I thought I'd be dead by the time I was twenty-one.

I almost got killed shortly after turning twenty in some gunfire at a club. A scuffle broke out between a couple of guys, and one spun around, firing a gun right near my face. There I was watching sparks flying off the end of the bullets. My first reaction was to run, so I flew out of the club and dove behind a car where another guy was hiding. I thought he was running, too, but I quickly learned he was the guy shooting at the man in the club. Out of all the cars I could have hidden behind, I picked the wrong one! All I could do was take off running again because I wasn't gonna be a sitting target.

After that incident I started getting tired of my life. I really didn't care if I lived or died. The way I saw it, there was no purpose to my life, no real reason to live. Plus my nightmare of the guy with the gun was getting more intense. For the first time, I tried to interpret my dream. After thinking about it hard, what came to my mind was the sun shining brightly down on me must have been God. The message seemed to be if I kept my eyes on God, I'd be able to avoid danger. But I also felt my luck was gonna run out at some point. God would stop communicating with me, and I'd finally get shot. Now that really made me feel hopeless.

The only ray of hope during that season in my life was the birth of my goddaughter. She was my friend's baby and like a daughter to me. Being that my father wasn't around when I was coming up, I wanted to be there for her. The first time I held my goddaughter in my arms, I got such a good feeling inside. I broke down and started crying, and to me that was a sign. My heart had become so hardened that when I held an innocent child, all the softness buried deep inside came out. My goddaughter made me think about my life and also about God. I figured if there was a God who created her and all of us, there had to be more to life than what I was into. All I'd seen was death and violence around me, and that wasn't worth living for. But my goddaughter gave me a reason to live. She and my interpretation of the dream were why I started seeking God.

I had heard about one particular church that was supposed to be pretty good, so I visited there a couple of times. One Sunday I was sitting in the pew and thinking out loud: "God, I don't really know You or this Jesus cat, but if You just let me live, just give me breath in my lungs and let me keep it, I'll do whatever you want me to do."

Shortly after that I gave my life to God. It was in August 1993. I did it at an eleven o'clock Sunday service, and the church was crowded that day. Because I'd been at a club most of the night and early morning before, I wasn't expecting any special blessing. After the sermon, the pastor called people up to be saved— you know, give their lives to Christ—and a girl next to me tapped me on the shoulder.

"Are you saved?" she asked.

I wanted to lie and tell her yeah because as much as I wanted to get saved, I felt like a hypocrite. I knew that getting saved wasn't gonna make me clean up my life, my mouth, or treat women any better. My thinking was that I needed to get myself together before I gave my life to God. But for some reason I couldn't lie to her. She was looking right at me.

"No, I'm not saved," I told her.

"Would you like to go up?"

By that time, all the people who had walked to the front of the church were being led to a separate room. She told me we could go there, too, and for some reason I followed her. Everybody in the room joined hands and formed a circle. We repeated the Salvation Prayer, which was led by one of the deacons in the church. That's the prayer you say acknowledging you're a sinner and that you need a savior. When you welcome Jesus into your heart, He becomes your personal Savior.

But even after saying the prayer, I still felt guilty. With all the bad stuff I'd done in my life, I was thinking that God might kill me.

That day I decided there were certain things I wasn't gonna do anymore. When you first give your life to God, you think everything is gonna get better, yet it seems like it gets worse. That's because the devil starts trying real hard to pull you away from the Lord. Even after Jesus got baptized in the Bible, He was led into the wilderness to be tempted. Of course, He passed all His tests, but I sure didn't. I struggled with a lot of things my first year and a half of being saved.

"Man, there ain't no way you of all people are gonna be into God and talking about your being saved," a friend of mine told me. Every time I made a mistake, people would throw it right in my face. They knew I was saved but still doing everything I'd done before like cursing at people and having lots of ladies.

"Yeah, you're right. I'm not there yet," I'd say.

After a while I made the commitment to get involved in a Bible study class and a men's group at my church. I found that the more I read the Bible and was around people who were into God, the stronger my relationship with Jesus got and the more I was able to resist temptations. In some ways my spiritual walk had been like my college football career: It had advances and setbacks. Each fall I'd start off strong and be on course to break rushing records. Then all of a sudden I'd get injured and be out for the rest of the season.

The first football game of my senior year was the best game of my career. Some said I would definitely be going to the pros and maybe even get the Heisman Trophy. That's an award that goes to the best college football player in America. But the very next game, a whole pile of guys I was blocking for fell on the back of my leg. My ankle was twisted around so bad that parts of my bone chipped, and I strained my Achilles tendon. I tried to play the very next game, but my ankle was so swollen it was hanging over the top of my shoe. I was out for the remainder of the season.

The good thing about that time in my life is that I was truly seeking God. Because of my ankle, I had more time to do everything, and I used most of it to pray. I was starting to develop a strong faith in God and beginning to recognize His voice in my head. By the end of the season I believed my ankle was healed. My coach wanted me to stay in college and play for him a fifth year. But I was hearing something different from God.

"Go into the NFL. Leave college," God said.

So I decided to pursue the NFL. Now nothing statistically, morally, or NFL correct led me to believe that I was gonna make it in the pros. The only thing I had to go on was what God had spoken to me. My going into the NFL is not what anyone had in mind.

"What about the boneheaded decision Curtis Martin is making to go into the NFL?" a sports commentator said on TV one day.

To make matters worse, my coach showed me letters he'd received. Different NFL teams said they wouldn't consider me because of my injury. But I was believing God. I knew I was following what He had said to me. That's what I held on to when my world suddenly started falling apart. First, I lost my apartment because the school would no longer pay for it. Then, I was in trouble academically because I hadn't been going to class (due to my own laziness). Next I lost my car, then my girlfriend. Someone even stole my pager!

"Well, God, right now I'm down to zero," I remember praying. "I don't even have a dollar. I don't have anything, but I don't even care. God, if I have to be homeless and Your purpose for me in life is to just touch one other homeless person, I'm content with that and will die happy."

When I said that to God, I was serious because I really trusted Him. "God, everything that happens from here on out, I will have no one to blame but You."

I meant that in a good sense. I had seen how, when I tried to control everything, it got me into trouble. So I decided to let go and let God take over. My hope was completely in Him.

Shortly after I announced that I wasn't returning to college to play a fifth year, an agent called me up. He said he was struck by my faith, and he wanted to help me get into the NFL. I think the agent believed in the God in me more than my actual talent.

He suggested I go to a rehabilitation center, and he made all of the arrangements. I ended up going to a really secluded place in the middle of the woods in a town called Sharon, Pennsylvania.

Day after day I worked out hard with a professional trainer. When I wasn't pumping iron, I was taking in the Word of God. Every day I would get up, pray, study the Bible, then go work out at the rehab place. Then I'd grab a bite to eat, go back to my hotel, and study the Bible some more. The only thing I'd watch on TV were Bible movies I rented. The only thing I'd listen to was gospel music. I wouldn't even talk on the telephone except for a rare call. All of this I did for two months. It was one of the greatest spiritual experiences of my life. Looking back, I was doing both physical weight lifting and spiritual weight lifting. I was strengthening my body's muscles and my spiritual muscles. When I left that center, I felt like I was glowing. I felt like a new person with a new reason to live.

During my time in the woods, I came to know God in an intimate way, and I learned to trust Him completely. In my heart I decided that no matter what I had to do, I'd fulfill God's purpose for my life, whatever that was. And no devil, no high water, nothing, not even me, would be able to stop that from happening. I was following God. I had a reason to live, and it was more than just surviving and more than my own goddaughter. I knew my reason for living was greater: to fulfill God's purpose for my life.

Two months later I was drafted into the NFL by the New England Patriots. By the end of the season, I was chosen as the NFL 1995 Rookie of the Year. My first year in the pros I received the title for best rusher in the league. Now that was nothing but God!

Today I'm known for football more than anything else. But the reason I'm alive is God. He's my reason for living, and I'll never forget that. Back in 1993 just before I got saved, I had made one request to Him: just to let me live and keep breathing. God has gone *way* beyond what I even imagined, so much more than breathing. Everything else for me beyond living is extra. All the money I've made, all the fame I've had, even playing football in the pros, I count as extra.

Football has taught me a lot. I've learned how to work hard, be diligent, and have strong faith. I have to have faith every day to go out there at 205 pounds knowing that eleven 350-pound guys are all coming after me. But I'm clear that God is the One who protects me on the field just like He did when I was in the streets. Looking back, I know He protected me all along—in my dreams, in that car chase, and in the middle of gunfire.

My life shows that no matter who you are, no matter where you are, no matter what you've been through, God is the same God to all of us. If you open up your heart, God can help you deal with yourself. He can bring you from where you presently are into a better, much more peaceful place. Many people are just looking for peace in their lives. God can bring that peace all of us want.

I believe we're where we are because of the choices we have made in life. If we can learn to choose God, we'll see where that can take us. Whereas if we don't choose God, we're choosing evil or wrong and that's where it will lead us. A lot of people say they want to change their lives, and they instantly expect a change. But changing your life really starts with changing your thoughts. The more I followed God, the more He helped me develop godly thoughts. That changed my attitude and then my behavior. And that's what changed my life. God took away my confusion and fears. He can do that for all of us if we allow Him.

 **CURTIS MARTIN** is a running back for the New York Jets. In 1995, he was chosen as the NFL Rookie of the Year. When he was with the New England Patriots, he played in one Super Bowl. Martin exhibits the peace and humility of Jesus Christ on and off the field. He is a member of Faith Restoration Ministries in Pittsburgh and also attends Christian Life Center in Brooklyn, New York. Martin is the founder of the Curtis Martin Job Foundation, a philanthropic organization through which God enables him to bless others.

---

1. Name changed to protect privacy.

THE MIRACLE BABY
Sharon L. Narcisse

Written by Sharon L. Narcisse

T he open coat hanger slashed across my back, ripping into my
flesh. It burned and scarred like a branding iron.

My life with my husband was a stream of abuse—from beatings and rape to even being urinated upon. This time he wanted
to beat me into confessing an affair with our neighbor.

He strutted around the bed as I curled in the middle, pulling
every inch of my body into a ball. This angered him more. The
blows landed under my breast, across my back and legs and any
uncovered spot my hands couldn't protect. My only concern was
that he not harm the precious baby in my womb. I was nearly nine
months pregnant.

My mother's personal prayers welled up inside me. *God, if
You're real, please help me escape this hell,* I silently prayed.

"Please stop!" I begged my husband, wondering why I even
stayed with him.

There he stood, blowing a thick, white, magical cloud of
smoke into my face. But the crack wasn't really magical. It was a

black, malignant disease consuming us. That's why I was so dependent on him—my drug addiction. I was a stone-cold junkie whose "daily food groups" were crack, alcohol, and marijuana.

To my surprise, he paused and passed me the crack pipe. Was this a trick to beat on me more? I reached for it, my hand trembling uncontrollably.

Then I forgot my burning gashes. I wanted to smoke that pipe more than being rescued by a knight in shining armor. Clutching it, I eased my way to the edge of the bed and fled toward the bathroom.

Locked inside, I heard no response. My husband had apparently decided to give me a break, maybe because his hand was tired. We'd been up two days without sleep, food, or fluids. I leaned on the sink to light the pipe as my baby moved. I gripped the pipe in one hand and my stomach in the other. At that moment, I had no idea which was more important.

What am I turning into? I thought, tears falling down my face.

I looked into the mirror, and to my horror, the room seemed to darken. I couldn't believe what I saw—the reflection of a skeleton. Dark, raccoon circles surrounded my sunken eyes. My skin was dry and old looking, lips cracked. Dehydration was wasting me away. I looked down at the trickles of blood oozing from my ripped, throbbing skin and felt myself dying.

Outside the door there was dead silence. *Is this a trap?* I thought.

I fell against the wall, my chest heaving with silent sobs. Then I turned on the shower to wash away the blood. The water felt like heaven running down my face. As I watched it run down the drain, I wanted to dissolve into that ring of disappearing water.

At last I stepped out of the shower, thinking, *Whatever happens is going to happen. I just need to get out of here.*

As I reached for the doorknob, trying to muster the courage to go with those words, I was hit with a gut-wrenching contraction. I fell to my knees, believing I was about to lose my baby. That was more than enough incentive to try to get out of the house. I touched the door lightly as if there was a fire on the other side. As I tiptoed from the bathroom, I could see my husband's feet hanging over the bed. He was capable of anything during his crack-induced outbursts.

Heart pounding, I hesitated. My stomach tightened. Another contraction. Man, I wished someone was around to help me. Many times I'd tried to get away and failed. This always made his next outburst even worse.

I grabbed whatever clothes were within reach. On the table beside those rumpled clothes was an enormous pile of crack. I hesitated.

"Take it. You deserve to have it," a demon whispered in my ear.

But another voice said, "Take your clothes and cab money and *run*. Leave that death alone." I followed the voice of reason.

Once I reached the front door without my husband moving, I felt almost safe. But that door always squeaked. Between watching for movement and listening for that irritating noise, I thought my heart was going to burst. Sweat drops blurred my vision. After an eternity, I opened the door. Of all times, it didn't make a sound.

Maybe God is real, and I can possibly make it! I thought.

I headed upstairs from the basement apartment in slow motion, my fear almost paralyzing. Even when I could see the street through a window, my neck tingled, waiting for my husband to grab and drag me back. A new morning had dawned. I opened the door and a gust of wind hit my face. My baby and I had a chance!

Shoeless, I ran for the curb in my robe, waving frantically for a cab and clutching rumpled clothes. Even when I was safely inside the cab and on my way, I kept looking over my shoulder for my husband to stop me. When the building was long out of sight, I laid my head back.

"Where are you going?" the driver asked.

"I need to go to the nearest hospital," I answered frantically.

The cabdriver watched me in the rearview mirror. I guess he didn't often pick up shoeless pregnant women in robes. Just as the cab pulled up to the hospital, the contractions came closer. I'm almost ashamed to admit my first concern was that they'd see my slashes and bruises. The doctors would call the police and arrest my husband. I told myself to hide it as best as I could. I really feared the consequences if he was arrested, then released.

Once checked in, I tried to put on a hospital gown without the nurse seeing my body. Despite my advanced pregnancy, I was a mere shell of battered flesh over bones. A grim-faced doctor walked in and looked me straight in the eyes. His words shocked me.

"Why didn't you consider an abortion? After all, you've been killing this baby slowly for nine months," he snapped.

Maybe because this baby could be a link to a happier time in my life, I thought. But there was nothing to really say in my defense. He was right. I began to cry from the nightmare of the past twenty-four hours.

"Why are you crying now?" the doctor asked coldly. "You need to listen to what you're facing.

"Your baby is at a very high risk of being born with multiple complications. There could be deformity and mental retardation, and, definitely, this baby will experience withdrawal. How severe, we will just have to wait and see."

I saw his frustration. I could tell he'd dealt with more than his fair share of pregnant addicts. Right then and there, I wished I were dead.

After the doctor left the room, I curled into a fetal position and rocked back and forth. I thought back over my life, wishing my husband were dead and the world had no drugs. But even that wouldn't change anything. The damage was already done.

What had I been thinking all those months with another helpless human being inside of me? During the past months, I'd sometimes wondered why this baby hadn't died. I even prayed to miscarry during one of those beatings to spare my unborn child a life of agony. Why was he still growing in my womb, holding on with his fragile heart beating, ingesting whatever scraps of nutrients came his way?

My hands shook as I folded them and closed my eyes, remembering the many times my mother and I had argued about my destructive lifestyle. She often told me that God is real, and He can help you if you just give Him a chance. Those were always idle words to me—until that day. They seemed to ring over and over in my head. I began to pray.

The nurse came to wheel me to the delivery room. I hardly noticed the glare of lights as I sped along. Besides the contractions, thoughts pounded me. When my husband was hitting me, my first instinct was to close my hands around my stomach to protect my baby. Why didn't I think to protect this child long before, throughout the pregnancy? There was no turning back.

"Push, push! Come on, Mother, one more good push," encouraged a nurse.

Suddenly, I heard a faint cry. "It's a boy," the doctor said.

I fell back, exhausted, and began to cry with my baby. Not from happiness, but fear of what I might have given birth to. I imagined a grossly deformed body, blind and frail, clinging to life. I pictured my tortured soul reflected in the face of my child. I closed my eyes and silently repeated, *Show me You're real, God. Show me You're real, God.*

I opened my eyes, and the nurse was standing there. "Would you like to hold your baby boy?" she kindly asked.

I stretched out my arms and took him. He was so tiny—less than six pounds—but absolutely beautiful! The world stopped as I searched his delicate body from head to toe. Nothing could ruin the wonderful feeling running through me—not thoughts of my abuse, drugs, or the danger my baby could face. I felt something I hadn't felt in a very long time—a stirring of hope.

The doctor left and the nurse took my son for testing. Reality was setting in, and I began to feel anxious again. As soon as I got to my room I called my mother.

"Mom, I just had a beautiful son, and he may have some problems. I'm really scared," I said, crying. Before I could finish, she was telling me she was on her way.

Soon, the doctor walked in. He shook his head as he looked over the report in his hands.

"So far, your son is doing well," he said, visibly puzzled. "Amazingly, I don't see any deformity or noticeable retardation. I need to stress, however, you must consider the extent of your drug addiction. The baby will certainly go through a degree of withdrawal. I caution you not to get your hopes up. The next forty-eight hours are critical."

Our eyes met. Despite his telling me not to get my hopes up, I saw amazement in his face and *felt* hopeful.

After a shower, I tried to get some sleep but was distracted by thoughts about my baby's future. *Will my baby suffer? Will he die?* A chill hit me as I waited for the nurse to tell me when I could see him again. I slept a little, but guilt was taking its toll. Despite my pain and exhaustion, I got out of bed and headed to the isolation nursery.

The nurse there smiled. I took that as a good sign. The otherwise stern-faced African-American woman with a gray streak in her hair did not seem disturbed by all the screaming infants. I watched her pick up a baby across from my son so gently and lovingly that I couldn't feel intimidated. My son looked so helpless lying there, tightly wrapped in a blanket, monitors everywhere. He was a month early.

I asked the nurse how the blood test turned out. She turned and shook her finger at me, tilting her head with a half grin.

"Sugar, there must be a God in your corner. And that li'l baby," she said, "everything seems okay. The test showed no drugs in his system."

What do you say to something like that? Did my prayer in the bathroom really work? Was there a purpose to this child's birth? Would he do something great in life? Will he change me? So many thoughts ran through my mind, but it all came back to one phrase my mom had spoken many times: God *is* real.

I headed back to my room, still counting down those forty-eight hours. As I walked down the aisle, babies on both sides wailed flesh-crawling cries. Some shook, and many had tubes running everywhere. Wow, was I blessed! But I wasn't sure why. Then the nurse came over and told me the doctor said there was a strong possibility my son would be moved out of observation to the regular nursery. I hugged her with joy and thankfulness. My son was a miracle baby.

Years have passed since that day in the hospital corridor. Thanks be to God, He continued to move in my life. My husband was eventually sentenced to a Christian drug rehabilitation program, PENIEL Ministries. I entered its women's program at the same time. God had an even better plan. It was there I accepted the Lord as my personal Savior and conquered my addiction.

Over the years, my faith has been tested time and again. But my unwavering belief that God *is* real and hears our cries and answers our prayers carries me through trials. I know mercy exists even for the lowest when we look to God for help. I saw His wonders right before my eyes, through my miracle baby.

SHARON NARCISSE is the founder and president of In Him Ministries, a consulting agency that provides self-awareness workshops and seminars for women. The organization's mission is to help at-risk women realize that they have the power, knowledge, gifts, and ability to develop into strong women through the power of God. Narcisse lives in Pennsylvania with her three children. Her teenage son—the miracle baby—is an honors student, an athlete, and an artist who recently won a national art competition.

THROUGH THE DARKEST HOUR

Dave Clark

Written by Susan Kimmel Wright and Sheldon Ingram

It was my darkest hour. From the time he was eight months old, my only son, David Emmanuel, had been wracked with violent and uncontrollable seizures. But that's not all. By the time he was school age, my beautiful, smiling son couldn't talk or use a fork and knife. Doctors told us David was autistic; his intelligence and personality held captive by a condition they themselves didn't fully understand, let alone have a cure for.

My wife gave birth to David, our second child, early on the morning of December 18, 1992. He was born in a hospital birthing suite. It was a short labor. Being in the news business, I was right there beside my wife, Rosalynn, and took notes on everything.

This is my wife and this is my baby, I remember thinking. I was fascinated. He came out red, head not misshapen, since it was a C-section. David was a quiet little boy, and immediately I loved him.

Our doctor, taking him out, did a quick little zip, zip with the umbilical cord. It had been wrapped around his neck, but when she took it off, David was crying and happy. And Daddy was happy and crying.

David's name was a revelation from Rosalynn. We didn't want him to be a junior, but to have his own identity. Rosalynn wanted him to be David Emmanuel because he was born one week before Christmas. Before he was born, she believed she would have a boy.

But within months of David's birth, my happiness had turned to fear. In public, I was a respected television news anchor. In private, our family's life was a series of desperate races to the emergency room and intensive care unit, wondering if David would even live until the next crisis.

If all of this had happened fifteen years earlier, the first thing I would have done was turn to God for support. There was a time in my life when my relationship with God had been strong and real—when I could virtually see, feel, taste the air around Him. But I'd lost that long before David was born. I went to church, but inside I'd been dying spiritually for a long time. I was as dry as a withering plant, desperately in need of water. My prayer life was hollow. I knew God was there, but I wasn't connected and had no desire to draw closer to Him.

My fears for my son did draw me closer to Rosalynn. She is a rock and an angel, and I leaned on her for everything I needed. If I hadn't had Rosalynn, I couldn't have handled my son's illness. It seemed like all we had was each other, but even Rosalynn couldn't change David's situation.

What do you do when you don't know what to do? I had no answers.

My life couldn't have started out more differently. You see, I grew up in the church; my family was a God-fearing, churchgoing one. I have two brothers who are ministers. Everyone in my family is born again. Church was a major part of my life. I was even a Sunday school superintendent, and I never drank or smoked. I loved the Lord, and my parents never had to push me to be active in the church.

In addition to having a solid spiritual foundation during my younger years, I was also into my career at an early age. I started out in broadcasting as a seventeen-year-old intern at a television station in Philadelphia. I left Temple University before graduating, then moved on to jobs in several major markets before landing my current position as a news anchor in Los Angeles.

Despite many warnings, I married in my late twenties, but the marriage didn't have a real foundation. All counseling attempts failed, and my wife finally walked out with our young daughter. Through the loss of my child and home, devastating financial losses and bankruptcy, I lost everything, including my self-esteem and my feelings for God. I was numb; I was angry, confused, devastated. All I wanted was for everybody to leave me alone. And then I met Rosalynn, an account executive for the same broadcasting company that employed me as a news anchor.

About nine months after getting to know this wonderful woman as a friend, God showed me in a single day that this was the person I should marry. At our wedding, I was so happy I could have run down the aisle doing back flips. I couldn't stop grinning and crying. When we were blessed with an effervescent, bubbly, healthy little girl three years into our marriage, we were so happy. But there was a cloud over us—the knowledge that I had another daughter who didn't have me in her life.

Rosalynn and I had wanted a boy and a girl. When David was born, my wife said, "That's all God makes. We've got it." After all we'd been through, we were so happy. We had our family.

We were going to church, but I was still just going through the motions. I just didn't feel inspired. Church left me cold. I would hear messages and look around at other people getting "caught up in the Spirit," but I didn't have what they had—joy.

When David was eight months old, we were living in a three-story town house in the city where Rosalynn and I met. Our daughter, Simonne, who is two years older than our son, was upstairs playing with David on a blanket on the floor.

When my wife went upstairs to check on the children, something was terribly wrong with David. His body was rigid, jerking. His glassy eyes rolled back in his head. He was drooling, turning blue.

Rosalynn called 911, and the paramedics arrived in minutes. They administered treatment on the spot, then transported David to a nearby hospital. I joined my family there. As far as I could see, David bounced right back. Surely, this was just a fluke. We didn't expect it would ever happen again.

And yet it did. I'd accepted a new job, and we'd moved to Los Angeles. By this time, the emergency calls were so frequent the paramedics knew our address by heart. Sometimes, watching little David go through these attacks was too much for me to witness. His face would often go through color changes, and Rosalynn and I had to watch needles penetrate every part of his body to keep him alive. This repeated itself over and over for six years. David was thrust into intensive care so often, it became our second home.

I believed in my work, but being a television news anchor didn't make it any easier. It was the job I'd always dreamed of doing for a living, from the time I was in elementary school back in Philadelphia. It's a fast-paced job and is exciting, as well as rewarding. I think African-American kids need to see Black men in these kinds of roles to help build their self-esteem and help counter some of the negative images we see of African-American men.

Now, as a television journalist, I lived by the pager. My son's condition added even more anxiety to my work. I didn't know when the next phone call would pull me off the news set or yank me away from a live report in the field, telling me to race to the hospital. David's life was held hostage by this violent illness.

His seizures, though, were only part of the picture. When we were getting him ready to start preschool, David was one of the most affectionate, loving boys, but he was woozy a lot, not talking.

We figured that was due to all the strong antiseizure medication. He was also behind on his fine motor skills, like holding a pencil and picking up small items. No one knew why.

A psychologist ran him through a battery of tests and told us, "Everything indicates your son is autistic." We'd never heard that word before, and we didn't know its full impact at first. At this point, it's something even scientists don't really understand. Basically, it's a learning disorder. Some people with autism are in a world of their own, or they can't cope with noise. Others are loving and interactive like my son, but, like him, they can still retreat into their own world. Autism is both fascinating and frustrating. Someone with autism might be able to play the piano but not brush his teeth.

Between David's autism and seizures, a normal life was out of the question. The doctors tried many powerful medications, some of them experimental, but none of them stopped his seizures.

At one point, my son began doubling over and wailing in obvious pain. He couldn't tell us what was wrong, but the doctors decided to operate. The surgery turned into a nightmare because forty-five minutes afterward, the doctor came to us and said, "Mr. and Mrs. Clark, he was on anesthesia, but he should be awake by now. We can't wake him up." At that moment, death stared us in the face, but miraculously, David finally woke up.

Later, David's doctors discovered David's pain had actually been caused by one of his antiseizure medicines. The medication had been killing him. We just didn't know.

In talking with David's doctor later, he presented another option for controlling the seizures—surgery to remove part of our son's brain. The surgery had been successful for some children, amazingly without destroying their intelligence or ability to function. But how does a parent make that kind of decision? I knew if the surgery went wrong, I couldn't live with the knowledge that I agreed to remove part of David's brain. Fortunately, we didn't have to make that decision. David didn't qualify as a candidate for the procedure.

Before I found that out, the question remained—what do you do when you don't know what to do?

Even at that point, I still didn't seek God's help. Instead, I leaned on my awesome wife. God, in His mercy, used her to minister to me. Her love for me and her strength for our family are tremendous assets. Rosalynn has exceptional talents. In addition to being an opera singer, director of an arts organization, and a business consultant, she knows CPR. My wife also carefully watched and recorded David's conditions and medical history. As a result, I depended a lot on her knowledge for David's emergency treatment.

Every day new problems came at us. It wasn't deliberate, but in hindsight, I know that I was leaning on Rosalynn for strength and knowledge and love, rather than God. In many ways, God still seemed far away. I was the one who kept Him at a distance.

As the years passed, my wife and I continued to wrestle with David's conditions. Through it all, Rosalynn was steadfast in her spirit and continued to grow closer to Jesus Christ. She'd grown up in the church and had given her life to Christ before we met. The worse things got, the more intense Rosalynn's hunger was for God. I still didn't have a one-on-one relationship with God at that time. I had too much garbage inside of me—bitterness and anger from my first marriage and the estrangement from my daughter, and bitterness from financial losses related to my divorce.

God used Rosalynn to get to me. She never let up. I love her even more because of her obedience to God and support for me. Rosalynn started to take off running after God, seeking His help while I was sitting around as a bystander. During the dark years of David's life, she wanted me to walk with her. She tried to encourage me to attend Bible study, but I declined over and over. Rosalynn would go on without me, and that would be OK with me.

My attitude was, "I'm behind you one hundred percent. Just go right ahead. And if I go with you to church, I go. If I don't, well, I'm still a good person."

I know she was frustrated because I was lagging, but she just backed away. She told me, "If you go, fine. This is what I know that you should do, but I'm not going to tell you anymore."

God used her in our home to set an example for me when I should have been the one leading my family. She became more and more fervent. My wife began to speak more in church. She sang in the choir and became involved in a variety of activities. I know she was praying for our family and also for me—that her husband would someday turn back to God.

And she was happy. In my mind, I wasn't unhappy, but I just didn't have any joy.

Even when I started getting involved in some things at church, I still did it grudgingly. I did it for Rosalynn. I know, too, that deep down there was a part of me that wanted to get back the faith I once had. But I wanted it without having to give up anything from my heart. I was too busy worrying about trying to fit into a new city and caring for my boy. I didn't even think about seeking God with the kind of abandon my wife displayed.

In the summer of 1998, my first spiritual breakthrough occurred. My wife directly confronted me. "I need you to be the priest of this house," she said. "I know God has a work for you to do."

What she meant was that she wanted me to be the man of the house by leading the spiritual tone of our household. So often, through neglect, we men sit back and let women take on that role in the home and in the church when God wants men to do that.

When I saw, in that light, what I'd been doing, the hard shell around my heart suddenly broke. It didn't happen in a moment; it was a process. One day, I got on my knees and poured myself out to God in prayer. I asked God to forgive me for abusing Him by neglect. I asked Him to forgive me for the time I'd wasted just sitting on church pews when I should have been serving other people with love. All those years, I'd neglected Him—not praising Him, not acknowledging Him the way He should be acknowledged, the way I had reverenced Him in my early years as a Christian. I was numb and cold. I had just done things—like ushering without any feeling. Technically, I had been a part of God's family, but I was more like a wayward child. Even if I was physically an usher or something, my spirit wasn't there.

I think this was God's maturing time for me. Through my parents, He had planted some seeds in me when I was a child, and those things have always stayed with me. But later in life, God allowed me to go through some difficult times. Still, He gave me an avenue to get back to where I once was. That avenue was David.

"God, you've already slapped me around, now open my eyes," I prayed one night. I wanted to experience God for myself once again. That's when God gave me a hunger, a desire to keep Him at the forefront of my life. He even gave me a yearning to join a church and become a part of its church family, which was pretty remarkable for me at that time.

At that point, I made a commitment to work to please God and serve Him. Rosalynn and I joined West Angeles Church of God in Christ. As soon as we got there, I could feel the people's love and welcoming spirit. In addition to going to church with new enthusiasm, I began to seek God in other ways—becoming active in the church, reading the Bible, seeking God's direction through prayer, and trying to be with other Christians. I'd grown up reading the Bible, but there had been times when it just seemed like familiar words. God had to break me down spiritually and remake me all over again so I could really hear and understand His Word. I also began to read a lot of Christian literature, which, for me, was helpful and encouraging.

Soon afterward, God directed me to a small fellowship group and Bible study for men, which had been started by a former NBA basketball star. Today, the men in the group still support one another as we attempt to be the best fathers, husbands, and community leaders we can possibly be.

In the midst of this season of incredible spiritual uplift, God began to nudge me and my wife to begin sharing our story of perseverance and hope with other people who were in similar circumstances or just brokenhearted. We began to do one-on-one counseling and speaking engagements. If people needed prayer, we prayed with them. If they needed a friend, Rosalynn and I tried to be that friend. Everything we did was part of our attempt to honor God. We are still active in this ministry today.

All of this ushered in a second breakthrough in our family. There were actually two miracles. They only happened after I confessed my faults to God and purposefully tried to follow Him. As I poured myself out to the Lord, I felt many of the burdens of my past—burdens I carried for many years—lift off of me. My bitterness and anger, the pain I held on to for so long, began to disappear.

As I followed God and assumed the role of spiritual leader of my household, God gave my wife and me a second reason to testify. It wasn't enough to say God took us through some dark times or a bumpy road or some generic trials. He took us through a painful, six-year ordeal when we didn't know if our son would live to see the next day. As I turned my life back over to God, David was beginning a recovery as powerful as the afflictions that once caused havoc in his little body.

The little boy we'd nearly lost, who'd come so close to having part of his brain removed, who couldn't talk or properly feed himself, now goes to special-education classes at school. He is finally learning to talk and can sing small words at a time. He now uses a fork and a spoon and is learning to use a computer. Soon he'll begin piano lessons.

David still has seizures, but only periodically, and now we're better able to predict when he's most susceptible. We believe that

his gradual and ongoing healing has been by God, and we're believing in the Lord for the complete healing of our son. My wife
is claiming David will deliver the commencement speech at More-
house College one day.

Six years ago, I didn't know why God had let this happen. During the worst times, I would say, "God, if You're going to take him,
take him, 'cause I can't keep going through this. It hurts too
much." It wasn't that I didn't love David; I just wanted to spare
him from further suffering. But God didn't honor my plea, because
David's illness was part of His perfect order. God knew the path;
I didn't. God has been working from the very moment all of this
began; I just couldn't see it. David's experience has been a blessing for our family. I can't add up how much our love for God has
grown through all these difficult experiences and how it has
brought us together. He's protected and guided us; He's blessed my
career.

Back when things couldn't get much worse, I asked, "What do
you do when you don't know what to do?" I didn't have an answer
at the time, but today my answer is to trust almighty God.

When my son was going through the worst of times, I was devastated. Sometimes when he has problems today, it still hurts.
But before I would just get confused and feel hopeless when David
was suffering. Now I deal with dark hours through prayer. If anyone is going through a trial, whether it's depression or raising a
child who has an illness, you need to know that God is real. You
need to know that He has power over our situations, and that's
what gives us hope. God specializes in doing things that we think
are impossible—miraculous things that even those we're close
to can't do for us. Turn to God. There's no other place to turn.

It doesn't matter if you're in a high-profile job or if you're a
millionaire; put your pride aside and pray for strength. While
you're doing that, thank God. Even if you cry, even if your knees
buckle, know that He won't let you fall. Just lean on God, trust
in Him, and you won't be defeated.

What really gives me joy today is going to church with my son. For the longest time, Rosalynn and I couldn't take David to church, because he couldn't stand the crowds and noise. Now he goes to church regularly with us and his older sister, dressed up in his new shoes and buttoned-up jacket. He holds his daddy's hand and walks calmly and behaves himself.

Recently, someone asked me, "Is this your son? I didn't know you had a son."

"Yes, this is my son," I said with fatherly pride.

Without God we can do nothing, but with God, all things are possible. Hallelujah, God is good! This is my testimony.

DAVE CLARK works in television news and lives in the Los Angeles area with his family. He is an award-winning newsman with more than twenty-five years of broadcasting experience. Clark's news reports have been broadcast nationally and internationally over such networks as CNN, CBS Radio, NBC News, United Press International, the Associated Press, and the Sheridan Broadcasting Network. He serves on the boards of several community and civic organizations and is active within the church community of Los Angeles.

2
THE GOD WHO MAKES A WAY OUT OF NO WAY

There are times in life when we hit a dead end, and our only option seems like turning back. That's when we need to pray to the Lord. Only He can make a way out of no way.

God did just that for the Israelites in the Bible's book of Exodus. Brother Moses, their leader, led them out of slavery in Egypt only to discover the Egyptian king was hot on their tracks. When the Israelites reached the Red Sea, the only way to freedom was through water. With no ships in sight, the Israelites sho 'nuf needed a miracle.

Well, Brother Moses stretched his rod toward the vast body of water, and God built a sandy runway to the other side. The Israelites crossed over safely, but Pharaoh's army never made it. The Red Sea gobbled up its men, horses, and chariots.

God made a way out of no way for Brother Moses and the Israelites. Today, He continues to part Red Seas in our lives. On the following pages, Christians share amazing stories of deliverance.

God is our refuge and strength,
A very present help in trouble.

PSALM 46:1 (NKJV)

GOD'S TIME

Tavis Smiley

Written by Linda Watkins

W e all go through challenging times in our lives emotionally, psychologically, and spiritually. For me, 1985 was one of the toughest years of my life. I was a junior in college and ready to drop out of school.

Throughout my college years I had been very aggressive about positioning myself for success in the world. I was a student leader and had hustled like nobody's business to make all the right connections at conferences. I had interned for the president of my university and the mayor of Bloomington, Indiana. The problem was, by the time I reached my junior year, I was burned out and bored. I believed I had done everything I was supposed to do, and now it was time to get a job.

But I still had a year of school to go. That was my dilemma. As much as I wanted out of college, I didn't want to leave without first getting a degree. But I definitely needed a change, and I needed it then.

To make matters worse, my parents were planning to divorce.

The news shocked me because I wasn't aware that they had any marital problems. I had never seen them openly fight. To me, their marriage seemed quite normal, and our family appeared to be a model of faithfulness in the Pentecostal church. When I was growing up, my family was in church seven days a week. I went to everything from prayer meetings and choir rehearsals to Bible studies and Sunday morning services. My mother was a missionary and later became a preacher. My father was a faithful, hard-working man. So the news of my parents' divorce shattered my image of my family. It probably changed other people's views, too, because the Pentecostal church frowns on divorce.

But my biggest concern was the impact my parents' split would have on my seven younger brothers. My two older sisters and I had grown up with two parents and knew the importance of having a mother and father around. I never imagined my brothers might grow up in a single-parent household. That happened with other families but not mine. The thought of it was very painful.

In the midst of my family and school problems, a trip to Los Angeles came right on time. In mid-January I went to a national conference of Christian student leaders. There I met a friend of a friend who gave me an alternative to dropping out of school.

"Leave for a semester and set up an internship for which you can get credit, and apply that toward your degree," he suggested.

"Good idea," I replied. "But if I do that, there's only one guy in the world I'd want to do an internship with."

"Who's that?"

"Tom Bradley, mayor of Los Angeles."

"Funny, I know Tom Bradley," he said.

Now that was the Lord working. It just so happened my new acquaintance used to work for Mayor Bradley, who is now deceased. I was a big-time fan of the mayor for a couple of reasons. One, because in 1984, he hosted the Olympic games in Los Angeles, and they were great. Tom Bradley—a Black man—showed the world how to host the Olympic games without violence and financial ruin. I was impressed with his fiscal responsibility and management skills. The mayor also was a member of Kappa Alpha Psi Fraternity, and so am I.

My friend's friend encouraged me to pull together a résumé and letter, then promised to deliver them to Mayor Bradley's office. As soon as I got back to Indiana I typed them up and mailed them off. There starts the saga.

For the next eight months, literally every day, I was either phoning my acquaintance, the mayor's office, or writing a letter to try to get that internship. At times my friend's friend probably regretted he ever met me because I called him so much. As you may know, the wheels of bureaucracy grind very slowly. My messages and letters were obviously being passed around from office to office in Los Angeles.

"We'll get back to you. . . .We're working on it. . . .We'll let you know if we're considering you," were responses I got each month. I was offended because I wasn't used to being put on hold. I was a successful young man who worked hard and usually got whatever I pursued. At least everybody in the mayor's office knew who Tavis Smiley was. I was the persistent kid from Indiana who was hounding them all the time. I had spent hundreds of dollars on phone calls. Three times I even used part of my college scholarship money to fly to Los Angeles to try to meet with the mayor in person. But three times the security guards at LA's City Hall refused to let me see the mayor because I didn't have an appointment.

"You don't understand; I'm here to talk with the mayor about an internship," I told them. But they looked at me like I was some kind of crazy kid.

I still held tightly to my dream, though, because I really wanted to do the internship with Mayor Bradley, and the pain of my parents' divorce was tearing me up. So I made a decision to direct all of my energies toward something that was positive, something that would take me away from my parents' split. That's why I put all my hope into the internship. I didn't want to go back to school in the fall nor had I made plans to return, so I really needed this internship to come through.

After eight months of writing, calling, trying to visit, and being frustrated to no end, I still hadn't heard a thing. It was early August, and four of my younger brothers came to visit me for the last part of their summer vacation. Everybody in my family knew I was vying for the internship, and they knew I was waiting for a letter. So my brothers helped me check the mail and alerted me whenever special envelopes arrived.

One day while I was outside washing my car, one of my brothers came running up the driveway with a letter in his hand.

"Tavis! Tavis! You've got a letter from Mayor Bradley's office!" he yelled.

So now I was just beaming. I'd finally gotten a letter, the first written response from the mayor's office. I just knew it was going to tell me that I'd gotten the internship. I had worked hard, been aggressive, and waited eight months for the news. So I grabbed the letter, ripped it open, and read with great anticipation as my four younger brothers gathered around me.

"Dear Tavis, We're sorry for the delay in getting back to you but we have no internships available at this time," the letter began.

I just broke down and started crying. I absolutely lost it right there in front of my brothers. I was frustrated and disheartened because I had invested so much time, energy, and effort into trying to land that internship. For eight months, I'd written letters, made telephone calls, sent faxes, and even spent part of my scholarship money on plane tickets. All of that to convince Mayor Bradley's staff that I was worthy of an internship that wasn't even paid; it was voluntary. I have a winning spirit and do not like to lose out on opportunities, so the mayor's letter hit me like a ton of bricks. First it was my parents' divorce. I had no control over that. Now it was this. After all I'd done, I didn't get the internship.

The next day, I decided I didn't want anybody around me. I

made arrangements for my brothers to go home. I was devastated, and even their smiles couldn't cheer up big brother. As soon as they left, I hopped in my car and just started driving with no direction in mind. I was completely numb and felt like a failure.

It was a clear, sunny day as I hit the nearest highway and decided to go wherever it would take me. Minutes into the drive I started crying and then wailing loudly. All the frustration and anger I felt about my parents' divorce and losing the internship exploded inside of me. Tears began to pour out of my eyes. I was totally unaware of where I was on the highway. All I knew was there was a huge eighteen-wheel truck in the right lane, and it was gonna be my way out of misery. Driving eighty miles per hour, all I needed to do was turn my car into that truck, and it would all be over. I was done with life. I was through with my parents' divorce. I was through with the internship. I just didn't want to live anymore. So without a second thought, I jerked my steering wheel to the right and welcomed death.

But the steering wheel wouldn't turn.

What's wrong with this wheel? I thought, jerking it to the right a second time.

But the steering wheel wouldn't turn.

Again I tried to turn my car into the truck.

But the steering wheel wouldn't turn.

That's what made me stop crying and take notice of what I was actually trying to do. I was trying to kill myself, but a force greater than me just wouldn't allow it. One, two, three times the force wouldn't let my car move toward that gigantic truck. After coming to my senses, I knew it was God. Only He had the power to do that. In the midst of my frustration, feelings of rejection, and irrational thinking, the Lord stepped in and spared my life! He actually stopped my steering wheel from turning in order to keep me from death. That's why I started thanking Him, praising God right there in my car. The result was I started calming down.

I just kept driving wherever the highway would take me, and

I drove for several more hours. I had no idea where I was until I looked up at an approaching skyline and saw the huge Gateway Arch on the riverfront of St. Louis. I had left Indiana and tried to commit suicide, but God had saved my life, and four hours later I was in St. Louis, Missouri.

Immediately, I thought of a friend who was the only person I knew in St. Louis. We'd met through the Pentecostal Assemblies of the World (PAW), a church organization. He and I had spent many summers hanging out at PAW conventions. Because he was older and more established, I looked up to him and trusted him. So I pulled my car over to the side of the road near a pay phone and called him.

"Danny, this is Tavis. I'm in St. Louis," I told him, breaking into tears.

"What's wrong, man? Come on over to my house. Here are directions," he said.

Obviously God was at work again because my friend happened to be home when I called, plus he was on vacation that whole week. He and his wife took me into their home and cared for me like I was kinfolk. They fed me, bought me clothes, and let me relax. God used Danny to counsel me until I got myself back together.

"That which doesn't kill you makes you stronger," he told me. I took his words literally since I almost died on the highway there.

Danny also quoted Romans 8:28 (NKJV): *And we know that all things work together for good to those who love God, to those who are the called according to His purpose.*

By the end of the week I felt so encouraged, refreshed, and refocused that I drove back to Indiana. Shortly after arriving home, I heard the voice of God.

"It's time to write a personal letter to Mayor Bradley," God said. He advised me not to write it like I wrote the last one, typed up formally and nicely the way things are supposed to be done. God told me to just get a piece of paper and handwrite Tom Bradley a letter.

So I grabbed a piece of paper and a pen and started writing the mayor a personal letter. This time I wrote it from my heart, not my head. I explained how devastated I was to have written him for eight months and gotten no response. I told him I felt like I'd been passed around his office and was devastated when I finally got the letter saying there were no internships available. By this point, I was so filled with emotion I was crying and writing. Tears hit the paper causing the blue ink to run down the page. I poured my heart into that letter, sealed it in an envelope, and lifted it to God in prayer.

"Not my will, but Thy will be done, Lord. I've been fighting for this for eight months. You know what I'm going through. You know my pain. You know that I need a break. You know everything about me, God. I think this is the right thing for me to do, that this is the right move to make. But if it's not Your will, then don't let it happen." This was the same kind of prayer I used to pray with my mother when I was growing up.

With that, I left my apartment, headed to the corner mailbox, and dropped the envelope in the mail slot. A few days later, the telephone rang and my roommate answered.

"Tavis, you've got a phone call, and it's the mayor!" he screamed. I was thinking he was talking about the mayor of Bloomington, Indiana whom I'd interned with before.

"It's Tom Bradley."

I took the phone, and it *was* Tom Bradley.

"Tavis, I got your letter," he began. "I want to apologize for how you were passed around my office. I had no idea you had flown out here to try to see me. When I read your letter, I didn't realize you'd done all those things. I want to do everything I can to help you get this internship."

Minutes later the mayor's aide called me, but he sounded much more tentative. "The next time you're in LA, come on by, and we'll try to set up an internship for you," he said.

That was on a Thursday. That Friday I felt compelled to make arrangements to fly to LA. On Monday I walked into LA's City Hall and personally asked for the mayor's aide. Because I knew his name, the guards let me by.

"Hello. I'm Tavis Smiley," I said, strolling into his office on the twenty-first floor.

The aide was absolutely stunned. He couldn't believe I had flown to LA. We talked briefly, then he took me downstairs to meet Mayor Bradley. Obviously the news had already spread because as soon as the mayor saw me in the hallway, he smiled.

"You must be Tavis Smiley," he said. "Come into my office."

Compared to my small frame, Mayor Bradley was a giant. The six-foot-seven regal man towered over me, but I wasn't intimidated. I was on cloud nine and felt like royalty sitting in his office. There I was, a kid, sitting with the mayor of the second largest city in the country, sitting with this man who was a giant politically and physically. Whatever feelings I had in the car weeks before when I tried to commit suicide were now just a memory. At this moment, I was completely in awe and absolutely elated.

We discussed the internship, what I was going to do, and how I'd get college credit for it. As I sat there listening, I felt rewarded for my perseverance, but more than anything else I felt blessed by God. I had worked almost nine months to get to that meeting with Mayor Bradley. Although we talked for only fifteen minutes, everything I'd gone through was worth it. The mayor called in one of his secretaries and started setting up things.

"I'd like to introduce you to. . ."

She interrupted, "I know. Tavis Smiley."

Obviously she was one of the secretaries I'd spoken to dozens of times on the phone.

"I want you to take his paperwork, fill it out, and get him organized because he's going to do an internship with us," the mayor said.

"When's he gonna start?"

"Right away. Tavis is going to fly back to Indiana, get his car, and drive back out here."

And that's what I did. Within seven days, I drove back to LA to start the internship. The mayor rolled out the red carpet for me. This was no ordinary internship. Instead of running around just doing busy work, I had real responsibilities. The mayor let me respond to some of his mail and travel with him to meetings. The biggest thing he had me do was organize the city's first Martin Luther King Jr. birthday celebration.

The event was a huge success, so much so that Mayor Bradley offered me a job after I graduated from college. That's how I got into national politics and eventually political commentary on national radio and television. My whole career sprang from God helping me to get that internship with Mayor Bradley and my subsequent work for the mayor. But none of this would have been possible if the Lord had not saved my life on the highway to St. Louis.

My encounter with God and the doors He later opened for me taught me several lessons. Number one is trust the Lord. Before 1985, the year of my encounter, I trusted Him, but not in the way I was challenged to when my world started falling apart. I was a young kid raised in the church who loved and respected the Lord, but I was also used to making things happen myself. But the internship was something that was out of my control. Even with my credentials and hard work, I didn't have the power to make it happen. Only God could move my unmovable situation. Only He could change my circumstances. When we've done all that we can do to no avail, we've got to call on God and trust Him.

Number two, I learned that things happen in God's time. They don't always happen when we want them to. In a moment of anguish, I tried to end my life, but God decided it wasn't the right time. There was unfinished business. There was more work for me to do. Only God knew that fifteen years later I would be sharing a message of overcoming and empowerment with a mass audience.

The Lord also knew the best time for my internship with

Mayor Bradley. It didn't happen in the summer or earlier in the year. It started in September, just the right time for me to get credit for a full semester's worth of work.

Third, God taught me that there's no situation that is so dire, that is so grave, that He can't do something about it if He chooses to. The fact that my steering wheel wouldn't turn into that truck on the highway was a miracle from God. My getting the internship with Mayor Bradley was because of God's intervention. It reminds us of stories in the Bible where God stepped into a situation and completely changed its outcome. Like the three Hebrew boys who didn't die in the fiery furnace and Daniel who wasn't devoured in the lions' den, only because God was on their side.[1]

We hear these stories so often that they're just that for many of us—stories. But in reality, they're examples of what God can do. If we pay attention to our lives, every so often we'll see miracles that remind us God is real. He saved my life and launched my career. He can also work a miracle for you.

TAVIS SMILEY, the former host of *BET TONIGHT with Tavis Smiley* recently announced new ventures which cross a broad spectrum of media outlets. Smiley will appear as a correspondent or regular contributor on ABC's *Prime Time Thursday, Good Morning America,* CNN, National Public Radio and the ABC Radio Network. Mr. Smiley's mission is to enlighten, encourage, and empower people. He is the author of five books and the recipient of numerous national awards for his advocacy work. Mr. Smiley lives in Los Angeles. He is a member of Greater Bethany Community Church where Bishop Noel Jones is pastor.

---

1. See Daniel 3 and Daniel 6.

A VISION IN THE NIGHT

Dr. Ben Carson

Written by Linda Watkins

B y the end of my first semester at Yale, I was failing chemistry class. My dream of being a doctor was about to go down the drain.

Obviously, you can't fail chemistry if you want to get into medical school. You can't even get a bad grade if your goal is med school. To make matters worse, I'd done so poorly that first semester of college, there was no hope for me. Even if I got an A on the final exam, I was still going to get a bad mark.

Fortunately, the professor decided to give some of us a break.

"For those individuals who are failing miserably, I'm willing to count your final exam double," he announced one day.

A glimmer of hope, I thought. *A very faint glimmer of hope.* I mean, why should I get a good mark on the final when I'd bombed everything else?

Looking back, I realize I'd gotten to that point by not taking my studies seriously. At Southwestern High School, my inner-city school in Detroit, I would study for a couple of hours before a test to get an A in any subject. That was it. So I wasn't that concerned about how things were going at Yale until the last few days before the end of the semester. I started realizing that maybe this situation was different. Maybe I wasn't going to be able to absorb it all in a day or two. The finality of my predicament started to sink in.

So there I was the night before the final exam, my hopes and dreams about to be shattered. I'd seen other people who'd flunked out and felt very sorry for them. But here I was on the verge of failing. It was so at odds with my self-concept. At Southwestern High everybody was always saying, "Oh gosh, Ben's so smart!" When I went off to Yale, our main newspaper, the *Detroit Free Press*, even ran an article about how I had the highest SAT scores of anybody in Detroit in twenty years. I felt pretty good about myself. But at the end of that first semester, I was groping at the bottom of the barrel, the low end of my class.

This is not me, I thought, trying to console myself. But then doubt took over. *Maybe it is me. Maybe I was just fooling myself and other people all this time. Maybe I'm not as smart as I think I am and don't belong at Yale.*

At that point, all I could think of was turning to God. My mother had such strong faith in God. She tried to pass it on to my brother and me, even raised us in the church. She taught us no matter how dismal a situation, God was always in control.

So I prayed real earnestly that night, "Lord, I always thought You wanted me to be a doctor. You know my whole life has been geared toward that. Yet obviously I'm going to fail chemistry, which means I'm not going to get into medical school. That means I'm *not* going to be a doctor.

"So could You please indicate to me what it is You really want me to do or preferably and alternatively work a miracle?"

I was very serious about that. Being a doctor was the only career that ever interested me. As a youngster, I used to listen to stories at church that often featured missionary doctors, and I was intrigued with the thought of becoming one. From the time I was eight years old, being a physician was my aspiration.

So the night before my final exam, I picked up my big, thick chemistry textbook and started going through it trying to memorize all of those formulas. Obviously that was an impossible task. But I always go down fighting. I never give up before the end, so I wasn't just going to throw in the towel and do nothing. Still, I was smart enough to know that there was no way I could learn a full semester of chemistry in one night.

Eventually, I fell asleep right in the middle of studying. It wasn't long before I started to dream. I was in the large lecture hall of Sterling Chemistry Lab. That was the 600-seat room where I had my chemistry class. It was a sunny day, very bright outside, but the room's windows were frosted so you couldn't feel direct sunlight. Several rows from the front of the hall, I was sitting in a hard wooden seat, you know the kind with the fold-down desktop? But I was the only student there. The other seats were empty. In the front of the room where a large stage stretches across an entire wall, a nebulous figure was working out chemistry problems on a blackboard. I couldn't make out who he was. I couldn't see his face or anything. All I remember was writing down everything he wrote. I was taking meticulous notes.

When I woke up early the next morning, the dream was so vivid in my mind. I quickly opened my textbook and started looking at problems I'd dreamed about. Then came the dreaded hour. I got dressed and walked over to the chemistry building, entering the same classroom in my dream. Only this time, I had to take a final exam, and my whole future depended on it.

I sat down in one of those wooden seats and opened the test booklet. I recognized the first problem as one I'd dreamed about the night before. What an incredibly strange feeling I had.

Wow! This is one of the problems. I know the answer to this one! I secretly exclaimed. Then I turned the page and knew the next problem and the next one, too, because of the dream.

Ecstatic, I shouted silently, *I know all of this stuff. I know this stuff cold!* It was hard to even contain myself. I wanted to cry out, "Hey, everybody, I'm gonna get an A!"

Obviously, I got through the test very quickly. In fact, I aced it. I was one of the first people finished, turned in my test, and practically floated out of that room. I felt as if I'd just won a gold medal. Later, I learned I got a very high mark on the exam and double credit for it. That took care of my chemistry class. There was no doubt God was responsible.

Before the encounter, I used to believe most of the things I did well were due to my intelligence. Sure, God was real, and you should believe in and pray to Him. But in reality God was out there somewhere, not an active participant in my life. However, the day of my exam, God stepped in and vividly did something blatantly obvious. It was like a Red Sea experience, where God parted a whole body of water so the children of Israel could escape Pharaoh's army. You almost had to be there to understand how impossible it was to pass one of those difficult chemistry exams.

After the test, I was meditating, thinking, and contemplating. I said, "Lord, You worked a miracle for me, which means You really want me to be a doctor. And I know You have a reason that You want me to be a doctor, and it's not just because I want to be one."

So I made a pact with God: "You will never have to do this for me again. I'm gonna learn how to study. I'm gonna know my stuff backwards, forwards, inside and out."

The whole incident taught me very important lessons. One was that God is there for us. If we have a mission, it's amazing the doors He opens. But He doesn't necessarily act at our beck and call. He expects us to do our part. While He's capable of working miracles, we should not anticipate them when it's within our power to do for ourselves. The lesson is *don't mess around.* Do your best, and God will do the rest.

I also learned God is ultimately in control and loves us. He's not willing to sort of sit by and idly let our dreams go down the tubes. Even if we've made some mistakes in life, He'll come through for us if we really believe in Him. God loves us so much, He'll even make a way out of no way. He did it for me. He can do it for you.

DR. BEN CARSON is the director of pediatric neuro-surgery at Johns Hopkins Hospital in Baltimore. Raised in a low-income household in Detroit, Michigan, Dr. Carson gained worldwide fame at age thirty-five when he led a team of medical experts that performed the first successful separation of Siamese twins joined at the back of the head. Dr. Carson is an elder at his church, a well-known speaker, and the author of three books: *Gifted Hands,* written with Cecil Murphey; *Think Big;* and *The Big Picture.* He lives in Baltimore with his wife and three sons.

THIS FAR BY FAITH

Lamont Couch

Written by Linda Watkins

I've always trusted God. Some say my faith in Him is a gift. I trust God so much that I'm crazy enough to step out and do whatever He says.

I left my job as a waiter in 1993 to go back to college because God told me to.

"It's time to go back to school. Pack your stuff and go!" He said.

So with twenty dollars in my wallet and no savings, I drove my '86 Buick Century to a state university four hours from my home. I had no idea what would happen once I arrived. All I knew was I trusted God. That's how I made it back into college, and that's how I made it through. My college education was one long faith walk, not year by year but day by day. It showed me that God is in charge of all things and how He makes a way out of no way.

I'd been trying to go to college full time since I graduated from high school five years before. But my lack of money made going to college almost impossible. On two occasions, I finished a whole semester of classes but had to drop out because I couldn't afford to go on. My high school grades were average and so were my grades during the semesters I was in college. That's why I couldn't qualify for scholarships.

Every time I asked the university's financial aid office for help, I was told my parents made "too much money" for me to get aid. That was ridiculous to me because my parents were working-class people. My father worked in a warehouse and my mom for the airlines. Sure they raised me and my brother in a suburb of Chicago, but we weren't typical suburbanites. We dealt with racism every day and struggled financially. That's why I wanted to go to college in the first place, to be a lawyer who could protect myself and others from discrimination, and to be a businessman with lots of money.

For white classmates at my predominantly white high school, going to college was automatic. But for me, college was a new thing since no one in my family had ever received a college degree. My father tried to discourage me from going. He never finished high school and had worked in warehouses most of his life. To him, success came by going into the military or by working in a "good" warehouse job.

"You'll end up going to college, fail, and come home with your tail between your legs," he warned, "or you'll end up graduating from college and working in a department store."

I knew my father loved me, but he was afraid for me. He didn't want to see me disappointed.

The other opponent I felt wasn't as well meaning. The main financial-aid officer at the university was racist. He wouldn't help me because he wanted to keep me out of school. But none of these things would stop me because I knew God could make a way.

Back in 1993, my life as a waiter was really hard. Along with seventy-hour work weeks, I'd sometimes work three weeks straight without a day off. At the time, I had temporarily put my dream of college on hold, but I was still ready to make a change in my life. So in August of that year when an old friend called to see if I'd drive her back to the university I used to attend, I welcomed the chance to get away and be in a different environment. As soon as we reached the campus, I knew it was where I belonged.

The next weekend I was back at home and had a dream. In the dream God said, "Go back to school." I was happy to call my job and ask for a leave of absence. Then I drove to campus, this time to stay. As soon as I arrived, I headed to my friend's dormitory room.

"I'm here! I'm getting back in school!" I told her confidently. She was happy to see me because we were like brother and sister. That's the only reason she agreed to let me sleep on her floor.

The next morning, I called the president of the university to see if he could help me get financial aid. It was registration week, the time when students picked out classes and paid their tuition. I was lucky to get a meeting with him that day.

"God told me to come back to school so I'm coming back to school," I told the president. "Now I know that I still owe $3,000 for the last semester I was here. But I want to be back in school. What should I do?"

At first, he seemed genuinely happy that I was eager to return to school, but after a short while he looked concerned.

"I would really love to help you, but the school has its bills, and they need to be paid. Your bill has to be paid off first, and then I can help you," he responded.

The president directed me to several offices on campus, but nothing came out of those visits. I wasn't discouraged though because I trusted God.

I was thinking, *God told me to go back to school so it's between me and Him now. Okay, Lord, what do I do next?*

"Well, Lamont, if money wasn't an issue, what would you do next?" God answered.

"Pick out courses," I said.

So that's what I did. I got a course schedule, read it, and picked out classes. I chose Spanish, English, African-American studies, political science, and health education that semester. The next day I rolled out of my "bed" on my friend's floor and asked God for more direction.

"Well, God, what's the next step?"

"Get books."

"But I don't have any money," I told Him.

Immediately, a voice in my head reminded me a check was coming soon. Three weeks before arriving on campus, I played a small acting role in a movie filmed in Chicago. The setting was a maximum-security prison. I was part of a prison riot scene. The thought of getting a check in the mail gave me confidence to pick out books for my classes. The estimated cost of the books was $320. That afternoon I received a check in the mail for $320! The film company had sent it to my parents' house, and they had forwarded it to my friend's address at school.

I was happy but not amazed because I knew God could do that and much more. What was different was how He was communicating with me. You see, for me, God had never been somewhere out in the heavens. He was always nearby, ready to help. Whenever I needed to talk to Him, even as a child, He was right there listening. But now God was saying, "You do this, and I'll do that." He was saying, "Follow Me," and He'd open doors. God was true to His word because a lot of people started helping me.

My female friend and one of my male friends let me sleep on their dormitory floors so I didn't have to pay for an apartment. They shared their meal cards with me so I didn't have to buy breakfast or lunch most days. Then I was able to get a job at the first place I applied, which is practically impossible for most students after the semester starts. I began working as a cook on weekends for six dollars an hour. That allowed me to give my friends money so they could get more credit on their meal cards. It was something to watch God move on my behalf, but one thing was still missing: Registration week was about to end, and I still couldn't pay my back tuition of $3,000 and my first semester tuition of $2,500.

"Okay, God, I've picked out classes and bought books," I said.

"What's the next step?" God responded.

"Go to class."

Now I knew how the school worked. The first week of classes, professors would check out their class enrollment forms and know who registered and who didn't.

"God, they're gonna be asking me about my registration. What do I say?"

"Tell them your Father's going to send you some money."

So I followed God's instructions. That first day of classes when professors asked me if I was enrolled I said, "I know my name's not on your list. But I'm waiting for my Father to send me some money."

Of course they were thinking I was talking about my earthly father. The school had no idea what I was doing. I didn't register for classes. I couldn't register. I just started going to class like I was a regular student.

I remember calling home to tell my parents that I was actually taking classes. I'm not sure if they really believed me, but my mom tried to sound encouraging. My father's silence on the matter made me want to succeed even more. To the average mind, what I was doing was crazy. But I trusted God.

Every day I asked the Lord for direction because hiding my situation began to get tough. When classmates asked for my telephone number, I told them I didn't have one. When they asked where I lived, I'd say "around." Then there were hardships of everyday living. I appreciated my friends letting me sleep on their dorm floors, but those floors got to be real hard after a while. Sometimes I'd be really hungry at night but couldn't afford to buy dinner. Other times I'd have to walk up sixteen flights of stairs to get to my friend's dorm room. In order to use the elevator to reach her floor, you had to have a key, and I didn't have one. So

I'd take the stairway up sixteen flights and bang on the door, hoping someone would let me in. On weekends after midnight the stairwell doors were locked. If I got there later, I'd have to sleep on a couch in the main lounge.

At times, I felt like a homeless person and wondered if it all was really worth it. Then I'd hear my earthly father's words: "You're gonna end up coming home with your tail between your legs."

Believe it or not, that kept me going. I realized everything I was going through was necessary. My goal was to stay in school. If the university found out that I was living on campus and attending classes without paying tuition, I'd really be in trouble. I wasn't trying to get out of my financial obligation. I was trusting God to come up with the money.

My church back home gave me $500 to help me out, and one day in October the Lord told me to write other churches for financial help. So I drafted a letter to churches explaining how much I needed and where they could send donations. I told them not to send a check to me directly but rather mail it to the university's collections office. That way they'd know this wasn't a scam. I decided to concentrate on paying off my back tuition first, so I told them all I needed was $2,500 more.

I found a national directory of churches in my school's library and was determined to write each one. Over a six-week period, every time I got a paycheck, I'd take twenty dollars to buy stamps and send out letters. In all, I sent out more than 500 letters. Every couple of weeks I'd call the university's collections officer to see if any money came in.

"No, not yet," she'd say.

But I was still hopeful. I figured somebody eventually would respond to a letter from a poor, struggling Christian college student. Out of all those letters, two churches wrote back. In early November, they sent a total of $500 to my account.

"Thank You, God," I said. "Okay, now I just need $2,000 more to pay off my old tuition debt."

By late October, I was going to classes every week and had joined the campus ministry. On Wednesday nights, students at our Bible study class prayed for me. That ministry was really important in strengthening my faith. Around the same time, I began to do volunteer work at a local Salvation Army. Growing up I had learned in church that if you need something from God, give something to someone else. I believed that. So I worked with low-income children and a Boy Scout troop, and also started helping college students.

For whatever reason, students I met on campus saw me as an inspiration. They'd often ask me for spiritual advice. It seemed like everywhere I went on campus, I'd get into a conversation that gave me a chance to tell someone about God. At that point in the semester, I wasn't anxious about money anymore. I was eager to know my next steps.

"I want you to study now," God said one day. "If you want Me to invest in you, you need to invest in yourself."

It was like God was saying everything I wanted wasn't going to come so easy because all through my early educational years I had played games. During high school, I was smart enough to get As and Bs, but I chose not to study until the last minute. So I usually ended up with Cs and Ds. That's why I wasn't eligible for college scholarships. As a result of God's words, I began to study really hard. I was determined to show Him that I was a good investment, and my work paid off. For the first time in my life I was getting As and Bs on exams.

That same month, late October, I met a Japanese student on campus. She was an attractive young woman with long, black hair who always wore a smile. I saw her in the library one day, then in my friend's dorm the next. We started talking and became platonic friends. She was an arts major and a Buddhist but liked to ask me for advice on different things. One day she shared another concern with me: What would she and her Japanese friends do over the four-week Christmas break? They couldn't go home to Japan but didn't want to stay on campus because the university was like a ghost town between semesters. Most students left, and there was nothing to do.

"Maybe you can come to my parents' house," I said.

I talked to my father and mother, and they liked the idea. My Japanese friend and two of her friends were willing to pay some money to stay at our home, since they would have had to spend a lot more to stay on campus during the break. They came home with me, and we all had a great time over the holidays. Their visit also helped convince my parents that I was really back in school.

When we finally got back to campus in late January, I knew my money issue was getting serious. There was no way I could start my second semester without first paying my old debt and first-semester tuition. I had one week to come up with $2,000 just to pay off the debt. For the first time since returning to school, I started having doubts. That week my English teacher asked me to meet with her.

"Okay, I need to put in your grade, but I noticed your name's not on my register," she said.

"That's because I'm not enrolled. I still need money for my tuition," I told her.

"Well, we've just got to do whatever we can to help you out. You're a really good student. I'd love to see you stay here. Don't worry."

But I was worried when I left her office. I was starting to feel discouraged. It wasn't that I didn't have faith. I couldn't figure out where the money was coming from. I walked down the hallway feeling depressed and headed toward the front door.

"You're going to fail and come back home with your tail between your legs," my earthly father's voice echoed in my head.

"Lord, what am I gonna do?" I opened the door and stepped outside.

The sun was unusually bright, and I heard people praying nearby. Loud praying, like four men were shouting from the roof of the next building. Their voices were so loud they vibrated through my body like a bass drum. I couldn't make out what they were saying, but one shouted, "Hallelujah!"

I thought someone was playing around with a megaphone on the roof, but when I looked up, nobody was there. I could still hear voices, but it was like they were up in the air. I looked around to see if other students were noticing the same thing, but they walked by me like they didn't hear a thing. Something strange was happening, and it was happening to me! When I walked in the direction of the voices, everything got quiet. All of a sudden I started feeling happy inside. My depression left, and I felt a deep joy.

Were those angels praying for me? I wondered.

There was no other way to explain what I'd heard and what I was feeling inside. I always heard that angels are praying for us, but we can't see them with our human eyes. But nothing like this had ever happened to me before. Moments earlier my spiritual tank was empty, but now I was filled up. My financial worries even left me.

"Everything's gonna be okay," I said to myself, then went about my business for the day.

The next day was Friday, the last day to pay off my old debt and first-semester tuition. I ran into my Japanese friend about four hours before the collections office was supposed to close.

"This is my last day to come up with my tuition money or I'll have to go home," I explained.

She responded, "I was checking my checkbook last night and saw an extra $2,000. I never used it from a trip last summer and forgot I had it in my bank account. I can loan it to you."

At first I wasn't sure what to think about her offer. I couldn't believe what I was hearing. I didn't know if I even wanted to borrow that kind of money from a friend. But a voice whispered in my head: "If you borrow the money, you can get back into school.

The financial-aid office can reimburse you later and you can pay your friend back."

At that moment I realized that meeting my Japanese friend was no accident. It was God's divine plan that we would be friends. First, there aren't a lot of people who will loan you that kind of money and it's no big deal. Second, my friend really wanted me to stay in school. I had trusted God for my tuition but never dreamed it would come through her.

She just happened to have her checkbook with her, so we walked over to the collections office. When she wrote out a check for $2,000 to pay the balance of my old debt, I felt like a little kid who was all nervous inside. This was actually happening. She was paying off my old tuition debt! The collections lady took the check from my friend, then turned to me.

"Okay, that's for the past. Now you have to pay for your next semester in advance," she said. "You owe another $2,500, and today's the last day to register."

Obviously, the collections officer didn't know that I had taken classes that first semester or she would have asked for that tuition payment as well. It turned out that because I wasn't officially enrolled in the school, I didn't have to pay for that semester. I wouldn't be able to get credit for the classes I'd taken, but that was okay because my new focus was on officially enrolling for the second semester. To do that I would have to pay in advance.

Another $2,500? Okay, God, now what do I do? I asked.

Like clockwork my friend jumped in. "Well, my parents gave me $5,000 for my spring and fall classes. I'll give you another $2,500 for your classes, and you can pay me back everything when your financial aid kicks in."

I couldn't believe how calm she was. She was so confident I'd pay her back. I wanted to tell her no, but I looked at my watch and saw only two hours left before the collections office closed. There were no other options in sight, so I started praying.

Lord, I don't see the money coming from anywhere else, so I think

I'll go ahead and take the loan. But help me pay her back. She's my friend.

Just like that my friend wrote out a second check for $2,500, paying for my second-semester tuition. An hour later, I was sitting in my new dorm room staring out the window and totally amazed at what had happened. It all happened so fast, so naturally. At first I wondered if it was really God. But the more I thought about it, the more I knew only He could make a way out of no way.

By the end of that second semester, the university told me that because I'd turned twenty-three and was no longer considered a dependent of my parents, I was now eligible for full financial aid. The financial-aid office, now under new leadership, helped me get grants and loans to pay off my tuition. On top of that, I got $2,000 a semester for living expenses for the next two years. Most of my living-expense money went to my Japanese friend. That's how I was able to pay her back. To this day, we're still good friends.

As you can see, my college years were adventurous. By God's grace, I never had to pay for that first semester, but He eventually helped me get credit for the classes I had taken. For each subsequent semester I was officially enrolled, I was allowed to register for some of the courses I had unofficially taken. But instead of attending the classes, my professors agreed to just give me the grades I had earned earlier. God also opened other doors for me before I graduated. One year I even traveled to Spain through a study-abroad program. I became fluent in the language and met my wife overseas.

In December 1996, I graduated from college with a double major in political science and Spanish. Then I went to a top graduate school in Washington, D.C., thanks to the support of loans. I graduated with a master's degree in international peace and conflict resolution.

My experiences have taught me that God is real and wants to have a personal relationship with us. He doesn't want to be a God who we don't know. He wants to be our Father who walks closely with us. The Lord also wants us to have faith, a childlike faith. That's a faith where we stop caring about what other people think and trust completely in what God says. When we have that kind of faith, He can make a way out of no way for us. No racism, low-income background, or person can stop us from becoming what God wants us to be.

My faith and subsequent academic success even had an impact on my father. After seeing how God had helped me, my father began to trust God more. When hard times came his way, they didn't weigh on him as much. I think he believed that somehow God would make a way.

Often I think back on all of the "what ifs" in my life. If I hadn't trusted God, I never would have attempted to get back into college. I never would have been able to pay for college. I never would have traveled to Spain where I met my wife. We must have faith! Our relationship with God is one long faith walk where we take the first step, and He takes the next.

LAMONT COUCH is an entrepreneur in the field of international peace and conflict resolution. He is establishing his own mediation practice in the Chicago area. Mr. Couch and his wife live in Glendale Heights, Illinois. They are members of Wheaton Christian Center.

3
THE GOD WHO HEALS

T he Bible is filled with stories of Jesus healing people. Folks with epilepsy, blindness, paralysis, and other illnesses constantly sought His transforming touch. Healings drew people closer to God, both faithful followers and skeptics who saw the incredible miracles and finally believed.

The Lord doesn't always choose to heal everybody. Sometimes He carries us through our suffering. Nevertheless, God is still in the mending business.

Through healings today of broken limbs to broken hearts, our Lord continues to reveal His power and love as the stories in this chapter show.

Great crowds came to (Jesus),
bringing the lame, the blind, the crippled,
the mute and many others, and laid
them at his feet; and he healed them.

MATTHEW 15:30 (NIV)

A WARM EMBRACE

Evelyn Stokes

Written by Linda Watkins

No mother expects to have to bury her own child. The thought alone seems to upset the balance of what's natural.

I remember the devastated look on the face of a middle-aged mother who visited the church I attend one Sunday morning. Her teenage daughter had been killed in a fire the week before. While members of the church gathered around her after the service to offer sympathy and love, tears poured from that woman's eyes.

Having never experienced losing a child, all I could do was hug her and offer words of support.

"I can't imagine how you feel 'cause I've never lost a child. But I know as long as you have faith in God, everything will be alright."

Little did I know that five days later a bullet would end the life of my teenaged son. It's a tragedy I wouldn't have survived had it not been for God's embrace, which went far beyond the human hug I'd given that teary-eyed mother.

Jonté, my only son and second child, always held a special

place in my heart. When I first learned I was pregnant with him, I was twenty-eight years old. I had mixed emotions about the pregnancy because his dad and I weren't getting along, and I didn't want to have a second child out of wedlock. But six months later when I felt Jonté moving around inside of me, my whole attitude changed. I was excited and couldn't wait until he was born.

I moved off welfare and started working at a job cleaning hospital rooms. Then I was promoted to a position where I gathered items for surgeons in the operating room. The moment Jonté came out of me, all of my sad feelings disappeared. He was a beautiful baby and was so big at birth he looked three months old. My son gave me so much joy, and I had such high hopes for him.

I just knew Jonté would go to college and be somebody important. He was a smart child and read all the time. I decided if there was no other man in my life to love me, my son was the one man who would love me unconditionally. Together, we were gonna do things. His life was gonna be good, not like mine.

I grew up in a poor family in Richmond, Virginia. My father was a cook at a veteran's hospital, and my mother did domestic work. I had low self-esteem and never really felt loved, even though I had two brothers and three sisters. Things got worse when my older brother died when I was nine. He was two years older than I and was the best friend I ever had. When he died, I felt like I had no one.

My family attended church when I was coming up, and I had my fair share of Sunday school, but I still liked to fight, climb trees, and hang out with boys. A lot of people called me loose tongued because I always spoke my mind. After graduating from high school, it was my smart mouth that got me kicked out of my first year of nursing school. I was eighteen and full of so much pride that I refused to apologize to a teacher after calling her a stupid lesbian. School officials said I could only come back if I apologized. But I wouldn't and lost my scholarship as a result.

Looking back, I didn't fulfill any of my dreams in life, from becoming a nurse to being a millionaire. But I was real good at taking care of children, and I always loved kids and wanted to support them. I loved my son Jonté most of all.

Several weeks before his death, I had a strong urge to spend more time with him. I'd always been affectionate with Jonté, but this time it was different. It seemed like I couldn't stop hugging my son.

"Hey, Boo, let's go somewhere," I'd say.

That's when we started doing things we hadn't done in years, like spending a whole afternoon shopping just for him. One day we drove all over Richmond looking for some sneakers he wanted.

About a week later, I started having nightmares. It was the same dream every night: Jonté was shot and lying in a ditch in front of some nearby apartments. The first time I had the dream, it seemed so real that I jumped out of bed and ran to my son's bedroom. He was lying in his bed with his arms folded across his chest like he was dead.

"Don't lay like that," I said, waking him up. But the dream kept coming back night after night.

"God, You're not gonna take my only son. He's gotta take care of me!" I pleaded.

For real, Jonté was the child I depended on most, even more than my daughters.

My son would do anything for me, no matter how tired he was. I'd wake him up at two in the morning and ask for ice cream for my diabetes. He'd get out of bed, bring it to me, then ask if I needed anything else.

I wasn't sure what to think about the dream, whether it would happen or not. Then another sign came: a sense of urgency to make sure all my children were in touch with God. Jonté and his sisters were baptized real young. But I had slacked off going to church for a while, so they did too. Around 1987, I recommitted my life to the Lord after God brought me through a scary operation. I started to attend church regularly again, but only my baby girl came with me each week. This disturbed me because I wanted all my kids to be around church people.

After the dream, I constantly prayed for all of my children to go back to church and put more pressure on them about it.

"Have you prayed yet?" I'd ask them each morning. Some days, I wouldn't let them go certain places unless they agreed to go to church.

I'll never forget the strange look Jonté gave me when I finally told him the dream. "You gotta be careful, and we've gotta pray for your protection," I told him.

"Mama, I'm gonna be okay." He sounded like he didn't believe me.

"I'm telling you, Jonté, before the sun goes down you *got* to come home!"

That's right. I set a curfew because in the dream his death always came at night. More than that, I began to act like a private detective bent on snooping out any harmful activities or influence that might cause the dream to come true. I was determined not to lose my son!

Only looking back did I realize and finally accept that Jonté was heading for destruction the last nine months of his life. After the dream, I noticed and pieced together aspects of his life that hadn't stood out before. One was how my son's circle of friends had changed after moving to our new neighborhood. Crazy thing was, we thought the move would get us away from crack houses and drive-by shootings. But even four miles away, the kids seemed troubled.

Most of Jonté's friends were basically good. They affectionately called me Ma Puddin'. It was his other acquaintances who were trouble. They were wanna-be thugs, thinking the bad-boy image was the way to live. The older brother of Jonté's best friend had just returned from a juvenile facility in Texas. He was nineteen years old and in for armed robbery; the word was he'd been in a gang. Another boy had such bad vibes, our pit bull bit him the first time he walked into our backyard.

"I don't want that boy coming over here anymore," I told my son.

But my baby didn't listen to me. He started hanging out with the wrong crowd and began to get in trouble. First, his principal sent me a letter saying he was cutting classes. Jonté was seventeen and a junior in high school at the time. Immediately, I confronted my son.

"What's going on? Why are you skipping school?"

"I don't know," he said with a shrug.

I was angry. I told Jonté if I got another letter saying he was not in school, I'd break his neck.

Still a second letter, then a third letter came. After the third beating, I gave him a choice: "Either go to school and apply yourself, or you're going to Job Corps."

Job Corps is an alternative education program where young people earn their GED and learn a trade. Jonté chose it over high school, and I was really surprised by that. But in three months, he took the GED exam and passed! The director of the program had nothing but good things to say about my baby.

That's why I was so upset when Jonté got arrested several weeks later. He and his "boys" apparently stole a car and got busted. All of them had to go to court and pay a seventy-six-dollar fine.

The whole thing was too much. I punched my son in his chest right in front of the police and almost knocked him down. I'd never hit him like that before, but I was angry and disappointed.

Then my son got arrested again when he was on probation. The boy with bad vibes was teaching him how to shoot a gun. The police drove by, heard the shots, and picked up both of them.

"If you lock up my son, it'll destroy me," I pleaded with the officers. By God's grace, they postponed his trial for several months. That night I beat Jonté to the point where I felt sick inside. When my son saw that I was having trouble breathing because I was crying so hard, he broke down in tears and promised to stay at home more.

All I could do was pray for his safety. I told the Lord, "I put Jonté in Your hands."

I continued to pray for my son all the way up until the morning of April 23, 1999, the day he was killed. That morning I woke up thinking about him extra hard. It was 8:30 A.M. and the sky was so bright when I walked into his bedroom.

"Let's go get some food, Boo."

I was in the bathroom getting ready to wash up and saw the strangest thing out the window. Our doghouse was completely covered with birds, like something you'd see in a horror movie. The dog was just sitting there all quiet. Normally, he'd bark if a bird was even in sight.

That's weird, I thought, but washed up and got dressed anyway.

A half hour later, my son and I were heading for the car.

"Mama, you gonna let me drive?"

Jonté'd been begging me to let him drive for a year, and I had let him drive once the day before.

"Yeah, I'm gonna let you drive again sometime today."

We pulled into the Waffle House parking lot, and I couldn't contain myself.

"Ouuueee, you look good! My baby looks so handsome." I gently hugged and kissed him.

"Mama, I put this on 'cause I'm gonna wear it to the job fair this afternoon."

For once, Jonté was wearing clothes that weren't hanging off his behind! He looked so nice in his red tailored shirt, black shorts, and black and red sneakers. I used to get so disgusted when my son wore baggy clothes. I'd tell him he looked like a hoodlum. But that day, he looked better than good.

"Your skin looks so pretty," I said, noticing a smooth golden glow on Jonté's face. It was really something because normally he had pimples.

We slid into a booth inside the restaurant.

"Go ahead and order whatever you'd like, Boo."

The food tasted extra good that morning. We ate Belgian waffles with strawberries and whipped cream, ham, eggs, and hash browns. My baby told me all about the job fair, how he and his friends were gonna be there. We laughed and talked, then drove back home.

"Now give me a kiss, son."

Jonté kissed me on the cheek and left.

Several hours passed before the telephone rang. My oldest daughter picked up the receiver.

"Mama, some girl on the phone say Jonté just got shot. But he's alright. He's at the apartments."

"What!" I jumped out of my seat. "Take me 'round there! You drive."

As we drove near the apartments, my heart began to race. I tried to look for Jonté, but my view was blocked by ambulances, a fire truck, police cars, and a crowd of people. A man and woman were talking to the police on the front lawn. A girl across the walkway was crying uncontrollably. I hopped out of the car and ran up the walkway only to be pushed back by a policeman.

"That's my baby in there! That's my son, my only son!"

"Your son's okay, but if you go in there hysterical, he could go into shock," a female officer warned.

Never in my life had I felt such pain. It was ten times worse than labor pains. My whole body was shaking, so I took a deep breath. Somehow, I found courage to try to get up those front steps a second time. Several officers stopped me again because no one was supposed to go inside.

"Who shot my baby?" Two officers grabbed my arms. "Why'd they shoot him?" I asked as they led me down the walkway.

When the paramedics brought Jonté out on a stretcher, I ran to my son's side. But he couldn't see me as they rushed him to the back of an ambulance. One man put an oxygen mask over his mouth. The driver let me sit up front.

"Lord, have mercy on my son," I prayed all the way to the hospital. "Lord, help my child! Lord, help my child!"

I wanted to hold Jonté so badly. I could hear the paramedics asking him questions. My baby was struggling to talk through the mask. That drive from the apartments to the hospital seemed like forever. We finally reached the emergency entrance, and Jonté could see me as they rolled his stretcher into the hospital.

"Mama, I love you," he said.

"I love you, Boo. You're gonna be alright."

There was no fear in his face. Just concern for me. It was the same look he gave me when I had trouble with my diabetes and he knew I was hurting. I found the waiting room and paced the floor before a doctor came in.

"Your son's vital signs are good, and he's not in shock. But the ultrasound shows fluid in his stomach, so we have to take him in for surgery."

I'm so glad a chaplain was around. She led me to a small room to pray. Meanwhile, family members and friends began to flood the waiting room. I was so surprised to see Jonté's dad. Apparently, the news traveled fast.

We waited hours before getting word that my son was heading into surgery. The two doctors in charge were so confident everything was gonna be alright. But I felt confusion and pain inside.

"You okay, Evelyn?" a friend asked.

"Fine," I lied. "When I get Jonté home tonight, I'm gonna beat his tail for being 'round a gun!"

Around 7:00 P.M., the female chaplain returned saying the doctors wanted to see me upstairs. My oldest daughter came along and so did Jonté's dad. I was stepping off the elevator when a sharp pain gripped my stomach. The chaplain led us to another small room. Seconds later the doctor walked in.

"The damage was extensive to your son's liver and major arteries." He paused. "We weren't able to save him."

My daughter screamed! Jonté's dad slammed his fist into a wall. All I could do was stand there . . . speechless . . . shocked.

"Sit here a few minutes," the chaplain suggested.

"No. I need to see my family."

I was clear about that. But it still took every ounce of strength I had to drag myself to the waiting room. The brightly lit space was packed with people when I walked into the room. I could hardly breathe but managed to get out the words.

"My baby's gone."

Screams and cries filled the space that was quiet seconds before.

"Somebody killed my baby! My baby never hurt anybody!"

I was so overwhelmed with pain that I couldn't even cry. I couldn't hug anybody or even stand up straight. Instead, I bent over at my waist, dangling my arms toward the floor, struggling with the worst pain I ever experienced in my life. It was lodged in my chest, which hurt so much. In anguish, all I could think of was calling on the Lord.

"Jesus!"

I pulled my body upward raising both arms in the air.

"Jesus! Jesus!"

That's when the feeling came over me. It started at the top of my head: a warm, soothing energy that slowly moved down my body. First to my neck and chest, and through my arms and fingertips. Then to my legs and toes. It was like a warm embrace. Everywhere it touched, the pain disappeared. I never experienced anything like it before. I was overcome with peace and joy, a peace that really passed understanding. Without even thinking, my mouth opened.

"Thank You, Lord, for the seventeen years You loaned Jonté to me! Thank You no one can hurt my baby anymore!"

Everybody in the room got quiet. They looked at me like I was crazy.

"Stop crying, everybody. Thank the Lord for Jonté's seventeen years!"

I couldn't believe that I was filled with so much joy and love for God. The Lord had touched my body and changed my pain into joy. If it hadn't been for God's embrace, I would have been filled with rage. I used to be a very vengeful person. Even though I had accepted Jesus as my Lord, I was the type of mama who believed in an eye for an eye, a tooth for a tooth.

When my oldest daughter was raped when she was fifteen years old, I wanted to kill the guy who did it when I saw him in the courtroom. Before then, my vengefulness almost made me kill my oldest daughter's father. He tried to choke me when we were fighting, and I cut him six times with a tin razor, slicing his face from his forehead to his cheek. He had to get twenty-seven stitches.

Vengefulness had been a part of my life since my oldest brother's death when I was nine years old. But after my son was killed—I was forty-six at the time—God's warm embrace took my vengefulness away. I was even surprised when several days after Jonté's death, a few of his friends came by to talk about getting revenge, and I told them not to harm anyone. "Let God handle it His way," I said.

Then when the boy who killed my son called to apologize, I told him, "I forgive you," without a second thought. Before God's embrace, I couldn't have forgiven him, and I certainly wouldn't have tried to stop Jonté's friends from killing that boy.

But God changed my heart and my perspective. Instinctively I knew that hatred and anger couldn't bring my baby back. I also knew the punishment was already done. Those boys have to live with Jonté's death for the rest of their lives.

You see, my son's death was an accident. His best friend told me how it happened. The boys had gathered guns to start a gang in the apartment complex. One of them was playing with a .25 automatic. He aimed it at my son, unaware that it was loaded, and pulled the trigger. When a bullet hit Jonté's stomach, all of them panicked. They called 911 and said it was a drive-by shooting. I believed their story and asked detectives to drop the charges against them.

I love those boys and don't want to see any of them hurt. I want them to receive the same warm embrace God gave me. Maybe then they'll get rid of their guns and stop gang violence for good. Mothers, we have to teach our sons that the most important thing in life is God. We need to tell them early on that guns don't turn them into men; God does. Without God in their lives, they are nothing.

We also need to realize that we don't own our kids. God loans them to us for a while and expects us to raise them right. I tried to be a strong mother and raise up Jonté right. Maybe if I'd been more strict, things would have gone differently. But I do know this, at some point our children are going back to God because they're really His. When they die young, don't cry. Our children have a chance to be with the Lord. They don't have to go through this evil world anymore. So let go of your anger—that's the devil trying to keep you down. In order to experience peace and joy again, to fill that hole in your heart, you've got to connect with the Lord.

The day my son died, I learned that God is truly alive! I believed it before Jonté's death but never knew the extent of God's power, that He can fill us inside and change our hearts and lives. Through His warm embrace, He taught me no matter how dark our day is or how terrible our storm, we can be at peace if we put our hands in the Lord's.

As a result of my encounter with God and the way He healed my broken heart, my pastor appointed me chairperson of my church's Comfort Ministry. Today, I visit people who are sick, abused, and grieving over deceased loved ones. I tell them from my heart because I know, "Honey, trust in the Lord, and everything's gonna be alright."

 **EVELYN STOKES** is a homemaker, a single mother, and a member of New Kingdom Christian Ministries. She sings in her church choir, chairs the Comfort Ministry, and works with Youth Ambassadors, a ministry that supports young people in Richmond, Virginia. For several years, she also drove a van for handicapped persons. Stokes lives in Richmond with her two daughters.

A TOUCH FROM GOD

Rev. Henrietta Sullivan Mkwanazi

Written by Salatheia Bryant-Honors

It took years to completely recover. For a while, I used a cane and took medicine. But I know for sure, God healed my cancer. My journey from a vibrant life to day-to-day in a hospital bed then back to restored health began seven years ago.

That Friday in August had been busy, but that was nothing unusual. In fact, it was just how my life was. My professional and personal schedules were always crammed with appointments and other responsibilities. I wore many hats and found time for them all.

I was an associate minister at the largest African Methodist Episcopal church in Texas and a guest preacher at churches across the country. I was also the mother of three children, caretaker of my sick mother, and an administrator at a county child-protection agency. Little did I know by the end of that day something would happen that would change my life forever.

I had gone straight through—not even stopping for lunch—diligently checking off obligations. By nightfall I was still going like the Energizer bunny. The last thing on my agenda was attending a wake. By the time I left the funeral home I was feeling fatigued. Not just fatigued, I was drained and unsure if I'd be able to drive home. Somehow, I managed to press beyond the weariness during the thirty-five-minute ride. But just inside my front door, I collapsed to the floor.

When I opened my eyes Saturday morning, I was in bed. Apparently, my teenage daughter and her friends carried me there the night before. Now 7:00 A.M., I was ready to face a new day and another busy schedule.

"What's wrong? What happened last night?" my daughter asked, entering my bedroom.

"Everything's okay," was my automatic response.

Everything did seem perfectly normal until I tried to toss my legs over the side of the bed. My lower back *ached* and when I tried to move my legs, nothing happened. I tried again—nothing. Again—nothing. I couldn't move from the waist down, so I began to reason with my limbs, literally ordering them to move. With no results, like clockwork, I began to pray for a miracle, even though I didn't really think I was sick. After all, I had too many things to do!

Why couldn't I move? I wondered. *Better call my doctor.*

Reaching for the phone, my mind searched for answers. Because I was anemic, maybe something related to my blood count was causing my legs to be stubbornly still.

"Doctor, this is Reverend Sullivan," I said. "Could you please phone me in a prescription to help my low blood count. I can't move my legs."

"OK, I'll do that right away," he replied.

But seconds after we hung up, my doctor called back.

"Did you say you can't move?" he asked.

"Yes, I can't move," I responded calmly. "But I'm OK."

Not convinced, he called an ambulance, and by noon I was at a nearby hospital. I had no idea what was before me. One thing was certain, death never occurred to me. I had too much to live for. After all, my youngest daughter, a senior in high school, needed me. We hadn't even applied for college scholarships because I knew I'd be there to pay for her college education. My mother also was totally dependent on me. She was paralyzed, completely blind, and lived in my house. Mother was the first person I waited on each morning and the last person at night.

God will heal me. He has *to heal me,* I thought confidently.

A few days passed, and nothing improved. So I prayed. Then a week went by with no change. So I kept on praying. A few weeks later, the pain actually intensified! My body curled into a fetal position, and the pain was so great all I could pray was, "Lord, have mercy." Once a young, vibrant woman, I now looked like an old woman. No matter how hard I tried, I couldn't straighten my body. Physically deteriorating, I still refused to give in to death, even though a dear friend offered to help me make funeral arrangements.

"God hasn't said this is it," I responded. "Until He tells me I'm not going to live, leave everything as it is."

Visitors came and prayed for me daily. My room had so many flowers, it looked like a funeral parlor. My pastor, family, and members of my church couldn't understand how I could be so sick.

Doctors were just as perplexed. At first they thought I had lupus. Then some said I had a bone disease. But I rejected their conclusions, all the time insisting God was a healer. I wasn't trying to deny my problem. I was too much aware of my pain and saw the sickness in my sunken eyes. But I believed I needed to express my faith by speaking the opposite of whatever the doctors offered. I figured if I allowed their words to seep into me, I'd never leave that hospital alive. Plus, I needed to hear myself say affirming words.

I told the Lord: "You have no choice but to heal me. I have preached on miracles from the Bible, how Jesus raised the dead, healed a woman with an issue of blood, gave the lame the ability to walk. Lord, help *me!* Lord, help *me!*"

Talk about tremendous faith! I just knew I was coming out of that hospital alive. To prove it, certain Scriptures from the Bible became part of my daily diet.

I'd say Psalm 121 (KJV) over and over. *I will lift up mine eyes unto the hills, from whence cometh my help. My help cometh from the Lord.*

Other times I'd remind God in Joshua 1:5 (NKJV), He promised, *"I will not leave you, nor forsake you."*

But August gave way to September, and I was about to enter October still languished in pain. Finally, the doctors told me they found a growth near my tailbone. They said it was cancerous, malignant. That meant surgery. At first I was hopeful, until they told me more than fifteen pints of blood were needed for the operation. Immediately, I thought about AIDS.

"No," I decided, afraid of getting the disease.

If it hadn't been for my son, I never would have had the surgery. "Please have the surgery so I can have my momma back," he tearfully begged. My son's anguish and pain changed my mind. I headed into surgery the next morning.

"God, help!" I prayed.

But three weeks later, my pain was still there. The doctors put morphine in my IV tube to try to make me more comfortable. But after months of strong faith, I had finally had it.

"God, if You won't take away the pain, take *me*," I prayed desperately. "I can't stand the pain anymore. Evidently You're punishing me. Please, God, take me. Take me out of the pain. Take me out of the suffering. Let someone put a pillow over my head and smother me. Please! Please!"

I was so tired of fighting. Nothing mattered anymore. I just wanted the pain to end. I told God, as much as I loved my mother, she didn't matter. And even though my children were my world, they didn't matter. The only thing I wanted was to see God's face. If He could promise me that I'd see His face in heaven, I was ready to die at that moment. That's why I prayed for death that night.

Moments later, around 11:00 P.M., I looked out of my hospital room door which was slightly open. A group of nurses were chatting in the hallway preparing to change their shift. Just beyond them was another nurse, one I'd never seen before. As I laid on my right side with my back to the wall, at my weakest point, she entered the room. She was a caramel-colored Black woman of medium build but there was nothing particularly memorable about her.

"Do you believe in miracles?" she asked in a gentle voice.

"Yes," I answered, barely able to speak.

"Do you believe God will heal you?" She walked around the bed toward my backside.

"Yes."

As she asked these questions, she touched me, starting at the top of my spine. She ran her fingers straight down my back to the tailbone and stopped right at the point of my pain. As her fingers reached midway down my spine, I felt both electricity and a sudden chill. It was an energy I had never experienced before.

"Oh that feels *good*," I said, gratefully. "It's like cool spring water and an electric surge going through my spine!" My body became so relaxed that immediately I drifted off to sleep. For the first time in months, I slept peacefully.

The next morning, the first thing I did was try to find the nurse who'd brought me relief. She literally lifted me from the depths of despair because I no longer felt like giving up or dying. The main thing on my mind was thanking her. So I asked familiar nurses to summon "the new nurse with the soothing hands." To my surprise, no one knew who I was talking about. They honored my request by searching other floors but couldn't find anyone who fit my description. Flustered, I began to cry. I really *had* seen her.

Then without warning, just as the night before, she appeared right by my bed.

"You're here. You're back," I said, relieved. "Where have you been? Everyone's been looking for you."

"I was sent to tell you that you will be alright," she said, calmly.

"What you've been through was not because of your sin but for God to get the glory. You're going to be okay. I'm leaving now and will not be back."

Ecstatic, all I could do was cry, this time tears of joy. Moments later, I drifted off to sleep again.

That was the last time I saw that nurse. Looking back, there's no doubt in my mind she was really an angel. At my lowest point, when death seemed better than life, she brought me a touch from God.

After our encounter, my condition immediately began to improve. I was able to straighten out my body, sit up, then stand up. I could actually take several steps after months of being bedridden. Within two weeks, my recovery was so rapid, the doctors discharged me from the hospital. I ended my five-month stay two days before Christmas.

Once home, my relationship with God became so intense. After going through a valley of illness, I became terribly in love with Him. It was like being in love for the first time. Early in the morning, before doing anything else, I'd greet the Lord. Late at night, before closing my eyes, I'd tell Him how much I loved Him. My new love for God was greater than the love I had for my own mother and children. Before my illness, I believed in God and had faith in Him, but now I was actually in love with Him. It was the greatest love I could ever imagine. We had a personal relationship that was new and exciting. It still continues today.

The whole experience taught me God is our total and complete source for everything. He's more than a doctor and more than life itself. God is the *ability* to even move our arms and legs. He's our heartbeat, our pulse, and our Healer. If we just believe in God, no matter how bad our situation, He will bring us through. God will restore our lives.

 **REVEREND HENRIETTA SULLIVAN MKWANAZI** is copastor of Bethel A.M.E. Church in Dallas where she ministers with her husband. In her role as copastor, she oversees worship services at the church, preaches, and teaches women's enrichment classes and a Bible study. In addition, Reverend Sullivan Mkwanazi speaks at women's conferences and workshops across the country. She is the daughter of a Baptist minister, the mother of three children, and a devoted grandmother.

THE MISSING PIECE
Ronald Tyler

Written by Linda T. Richardson

For twenty-two years, heroin was the god of my life. I started doing drugs in 1971 when I was seventeen and growing up in Baltimore. I already was drinking beer and hard alcohol like 100-proof Old Granddad because I was tired of being called square by my friends. Around the same time, I'd hang out at one of the neighborhood playgrounds and watch junkies get sick and throw up.

At first, that turned me off. Then one day a guy who was about five years older offered me some of the heroin he was sniffing. I started to turn it down, telling him, "Junkies die from that stuff and steal from their parents and all that. I'm going to stick to drinking my Colt 45." But my friends said it wouldn't be that bad as long as I was snorting the heroin and not injecting it. I decided to believe them and gave it a try. I threw up but also felt like I could conquer the world.

Soon it was routine for me to snort heroin in order to get high. That wasn't enough for long, though. By the age of eighteen, I was

getting irritated by the powder falling off the matchstick or whatever else I could find for snorting. Then a friend told me, "Man,
you're wasting heroin by snorting it off a matchstick. Why don't
you go ahead and inject it?"

That made sense to me. My friend showed me how to do everything from cooking the powder in a bottle cap to using a hypo-
dermic needle to finding a good vein. Like so many junkies I'd
seen, I continued to get sick and vomit. But like so many junkies
probably felt, I experienced a sweeping euphoria, a feeling of being able to conquer the world. While some junkies would nod and
drool after shooting up, when I shot up heroin, I would become
happier than usual. I remember thinking, *I see why junkies stay
on this stuff; you don't care about nothin'*. As a teenager, I was
hooked.

You might think at that age I had difficulty supporting a heroin
habit. But money wasn't a problem. A cap of heroin was only one
dollar, nothing like it costs today. My brother, sister, and I grew
up middle class and lived in a neighborhood where few African-
Americans had homes. My father worked for a shipbuilding company, and we always seemed to have the things we needed. My
mother even taught us that God in His goodness had provided
for our family. So she took pleasure in giving me a dollar here
and there whenever I asked for it. Little did she know I was using the money to buy drugs. When I couldn't get money from
her, I got heroin in other ways. Sometimes friends who ran drug
clicks and owed me favors gave me the heroin I needed. I never
had to steal from anyone.

My day-to-day routine of hanging out with friends, getting
high, partying, and fighting led to my dropping out of high school
in the eleventh grade. I was sent to reform school for seriously
injuring the eye of the son of a prominent Baltimore mortician
during a fight after a party.

I couldn't do drugs in reform school but resumed when I was
released. Again, money was no problem because now I was work-

ing. I worked for a cousin who owned a business that sanded Sheetrock used for building condominiums. On another job, I earned eight dollars an hour and traveled across the country, working with an uncle who owned his own truck rig. I was young, making big money for someone who didn't have a high school diploma or college degree, and I was wasting it all on drugs and parties. My life was going nowhere.

Seeing the pain on my mother's face because I didn't finish high school, I joined the Army in 1977. Fortunately for me, there was no testing for drugs during that time. I passed all the tests and began what turned into a career that spanned ten years as a weapons specialist who maintained small weapons. During this period of my life I also married my childhood sweetheart, and we had a son. But the marriage soon failed because of my crazy lifestyle. During our separation, I became what I call a "United Nations soldier." I had sexual encounters with women of many nationalities.

Heroin was still very much a part of my existence. I was able to get drugs whenever I needed them. I was an addict, and I didn't care about the risk to my job or to me. Ironically, my drug use didn't affect my job performance as a weapons specialist. I was recognized as an expert at what I did, and I did it well in spite of my drug use.

While on leave from my army base to attend my parents' forty-fifth wedding anniversary celebration, I witnessed the tragic death of my mother. It changed my life forever and still haunts me today. It was on January 4, 1983, and I was sleeping with my girlfriend in my old bedroom in my parents' house. At 7:15 A.M., my girl abruptly woke me up and asked, "Ron, what's that sound? Something's wrong. Listen." I was still hung over from alcohol and heroin when I heard a crackling noise. Instinctively, I threw my feet out of the bed onto the floor to go see if I could find out what was going on. When my feet touched the floor, it was scorching hot, which told me there was a fire somewhere in the house.

I ran to wake up Mama, who was asleep in the middle room next to mine. After waking her, she saw what was happening and started screaming for my niece. She believed she was in another bedroom. When I opened my mama's bedroom door, which led to a hallway to go downstairs, black smoke—the thickest smoke I'd ever seen—almost knocked me down.

My mother tried to push past me into the smoke to go downstairs to find my niece. I realized she wouldn't make it through the smoke, which by this time had me gagging. As we struggled, she shoved me, ran out into the hall, and disappeared into the smoke. In a panic, I reached into the smoke in an effort to grab her. My mother was Cherokee, with long, beautiful hair. All I could do to keep from losing her in the wall of smoke was to grab her hair, pull her back into the bedroom and close the door. My mother, my girlfriend, and I ran back to the room where I was sleeping. I lifted the window and yelled to my mother, "Stay on the bed." I had already called 911, and we could hear the fire engine sirens in the distance.

My plan was to jump from the second-story bedroom window, run around to the front of the house, and run back upstairs to rescue my mother and my girlfriend. So I jumped. But when I hit the ground, I heard my foot snap. I felt excruciating pain but didn't know how bad my injury was. I immediately jumped up from the ground, limping, thinking my ankle was just sprained. Neighbors responding to the fire pushed me back down, preventing me from following through with my plan to rescue my mother. I yelled at them, "Mama's stuck in there." Someone yelled back at me, "Ronnie, look at your foot; look down at your foot!" When I looked down, my foot was dangling from my ankle by arteries, veins, and muscle. The bone connecting my ankle and foot was completely shattered.

The last thing I remember was looking up at the window, where by this time my mother had managed to crawl out onto the window ledge. Everything was in chaos. A neighbor tried to detach a forty-foot ladder chained to his fence, but he couldn't do it. My godbrother smashed a lower window of the house to try to get in that way. Immediately we saw that the fire wasn't as extensive as we thought; it was in a small room off the first floor. I looked up to see my mother in the window and yelled, "Mama, get back in the window; it's not that bad." But she didn't have the strength to pull herself back into the room. All I remember is hearing a thud and a crack—the thud of her back hitting the ground and the crack of her neck breaking from the fall.

I went into shock from the trauma of what I'd witnessed and woke up in a hospital. The medical team rushed me into surgery to reconstruct my right ankle. Hours later, I woke up to find my leg in midair, hanging in traction. My arm was attached to a morphine drip to dull the pain.

About 12:30 the next morning, I remember waking up from a restless sleep. I started reliving the nightmare of my mother's tragic death. I didn't save her or buffer her fall. *I killed my mother,* I thought.

That pushed me into a state of depression. I didn't want to live anymore with the guilt that I was responsible for her death. I remember sitting up in bed, leaning forward, and removing my foot from traction, all the time thinking, *If I could maneuver myself over to my hospital room window, I'd throw something through it to break the glass, jump, and kill myself from the fall to the ground.*

I tried to ease myself off the bed and heard something, somebody say clearly, *"You must go on with your life."* So I stopped moving and looked around to see if anyone had come into the room. *"You must go on with your life. Your mother would want it that way,"* the voice continued. *"You have things to do."*

What the heck was that? I thought. The voice filled me with a sense of peace, unlike anything I had ever experienced. I no longer thought about suicide, only peace. I laid down on my bed and drifted into a peaceful sleep.

My doctor stopped by later in the day, and I told him about the voice that told me to live. The doctor said, "Well, you know morphine can do that to you. You probably had an hallucination." But I knew in my heart that wasn't the case. There were too many details I clearly remembered from the experience.

Because I was still in the military, several days later I was transferred to a medical facility near Baltimore. For the next eight months, surgeries were performed on my ankle, and eventually pins were placed inside to hold it together. Also, my doctor had been monitoring my moods and decided I needed professional help with depression. An ambulance took me to an Army hospital in Washington, D.C., where I spent forty-five days on the psychiatric ward for observation and rehabilitation for my ankle. I continued shooting heroin, which was supplied to me by friends. Finding drugs in Washington was easy then, and I'm sure much hasn't changed.

Eventually, the Army decided to re-enlist me, and I was stationed in Korea. Even in Korea, I was able to purchase heroin. Buying drugs while stationed in a foreign country was easy, yet dangerous. Overseas, narcotics weren't cut or processed like they were in the States, so you got pure heroin. Not only did you run the risk of a life-threatening reaction to the drug, you also ran the risk of being imprisoned for life, without parole, if caught buying drugs.

About seven months later, my commander told me there had been a mistake concerning my re-enlistment. I was flown back to Washington, D.C. for another evaluation of my injury. While there, a friend who had dated a woman I was seeing at that time told me that my girlfriend had given him a new sexually transmitted gay disease. He said addicts were catching it, and it was being spread from men to women and men to men.

I decided to go to a community health clinic to get tested instead of doing it at the army hospital. A soldier diagnosed with a sexually transmitted disease could be disciplined for destruction of government property. One night while in the barracks, I got a phone call from the clinic. The woman on the phone said, "We think you need to come down here."

A doctor at the clinic told me that I had HTLV. That's what they called HIV back then. "The doctors are doing research, but presently we have no medicines for this disease . . . Doctors don't know how to counsel or treat people," he said.

The first thing that came to mind was, *Okay, I'm dying, so let me go out with a blast of heroin. I'm really gonna party it up now.*

In the next breath, the doctor added, "We need for you to give us the names of all your sexual contacts so we can ask them to come in for testing."

The next day, it hit me: *What are people gonna say? They're gonna think I'm gay.* And I wasn't too far off. All of sudden, my popular image changed. Women I had slept with said, "You gave me *what?*" I got spat on, slapped, hit in the mouth. I had no choice but to take the abuse.

Things got even worse from this point. The Military Medical Board found me unfit for duty because of my ankle injury. They didn't know about my HIV diagnosis. In 1987, I was discharged from service. I was so angry and bitter at the government because I knew I could still handle my responsibilities.

They gave me $20,000 in severance pay when I was discharged, and I settled into an apartment in Silver Spring, Maryland. With the money I had and through my contacts, I bought and sold drugs. At my peak as a drug dealer, I was dealing thirty grams of cocaine a day at $100 per gram. I was selling drugs to soldiers, military officers, mailmen, waitresses, and my regular street customers. To throw the cops off, I had women selling drugs for me because the cops were hassling African, Latino, and African-American men. They gave Jamaican brothers an especially hard time.

The risks of dealing drugs became a reality when two of my police friends approached me at a picnic to warn me that undercover cops were getting close to having all the information they needed to raid my apartment. My friends told me to leave the D.C. area quickly and not look back. I don't know if it was the fear of the cops who had me under investigation or memories of my mother's tragic death, but I went into suicidal depression. An old friend suggested I should go to a mental hospital in Washington, D.C. I went there for several months of outpatient therapy. Then my case was transferred to the veterans hospital. I was admitted, and a doctor started me on antidepressant medication.

After reading my records, doctors asked to test me for sexually transmitted diseases because of my history of drug use. The first test results came back positive for Hepatitis C, a liver infection sometimes associated with drug use. It can cause severe problems, which can lead to jaundice or infection in the body. The doctors focused on treating the hepatitis and my depression. Two weeks later, my HIV test results came back positive.

I remember sitting in the dayroom at the veterans hospital when the nurse came in. "Mr. Tyler, the doctor wants to talk with you," she said. I went to his office and found him sitting there with two psychiatric technicians, two security guards, and a priest. I thought, *Oh, my God!* It was then that the doctor said, "Ron, do as much as you can, get your life in order. I'm sorry to have to tell you that your tests came back positive, and you probably have two years left to live."

Here I am thinking, *I've just been diagnosed with AIDS a second time. I watched my mother fall to her death from a burning house. I nearly ripped off my foot jumping out the window. I was put out of the army. All in less than six years. What next?*

After my release from the hospital, I realized my life's rollercoaster ride was over. I moved to my family's home in Baltimore, far from the drug dealer's life of a fancy apartment, a $4,000 gold watch, diamond rings, and a Cadillac Seville. I still used drugs, but I was thinking about my mother's death more and more.

One day I woke up to go get my fix when something suddenly hit me. I realized that I was meant to do more with my life. It wasn't like something specific prompted that thought. It just happened. I caught the bus to the VA hospital and told the staff, "I can't guarantee you that if I'm not admitted, I won't blow my brains out. I'm addicted to heroin and depressed." They admitted me immediately.

I was placed in a room on the detoxification and psychiatric floor with a guy who received regular visits from two men who were deacons at a local church. The men also held a Bible study in the ward. I would lie on my bed pretending not to listen when they talked about Jesus, thinking, *Man, they're brainwashing my roommate with this cult stuff. A bunch of Bible-toting Jesus freaks.*

One day they asked me to join them, and for whatever reason, I said, "OK." They gave me a Bible, and night after night I started reading it and thinking about the things I had done in my life. I should have died from overdosing, getting shot, or whatever, but I didn't. Was that because this Jesus wouldn't let it happen so I could do something special in the future?

I wanted to believe in Jesus, but what the deacons said about Him sounded too good to be true. Every night I sat in a circle with about eleven other patients from the ward, listening to one of the deacons explain that we needed to admit our sins, pray for forgiveness, and ask Jesus to come into our lives as Lord and Savior. Then we would all hold hands, and the deacons would start praying. Men went from saying, "Thank You, Jesus," to crying and shouting. I could feel the Spirit of the Lord flowing through that circle.

I started to see a change in some of the men. They stopped cursing. They seemed in awe of the internal, natural high they were experiencing. They interacted with one another differently. They seemed to know some kind of change had happened in their hearts without voicing it to one another. I was feeling the same things.

For the first time in a long while, I wasn't thinking about drugs, HIV, money, or women. I could only think about the voice

I had heard a decade before, telling me *"You must go on with your life."* I was convinced that Jesus was actually taking charge of my life, and I needed to accept Him.

So on April 23, 1993, while standing in a prayer circle in another patient's room, I asked Jesus to be my Lord and Savior. I was thirty-eight years old. When I went to my room that night and laid down, I heard a voice say, *"If you go back this time, you will not make it. If you go back this time, you will not get another chance."* It was the same voice I'd heard ten years earlier, and I knew it was God. God was letting me know that if I went back to my old life of drugs and womanizing, He'd remove the hedge of protection that had been saving my life. There would be no more chances.

That night, I understood that God gives us a mind to make choices, wise choices or foolish ones. I believed He was telling me if I ever make a foolish choice again, He would not be there to help me. The prayer circle, accepting Christ, and hearing God's voice was a true encounter with the Lord. That set the tone for the rest of my spiritual life. I know now that God told me in that room, this was my last chance.

After that, I didn't want heroin anymore, and I didn't need the methadone pills I was being given. It was like God put me through His own detox process. With His process, I didn't experience the normal withdrawal symptoms most recovering addicts have. I was looking forward to what God had in store for me after I left the hospital. I had been healed!

After being discharged, I started going to the church that the deacons at the hospital went to. I continued with Bible study there and also read the Bible on my own. As I began to grow spiritually, everything in my past became crystal clear. God kept me to heal me. Each step of the way He was saying, *"Nope, you can't die today."* I began to understand that even unsaved, if God has already predestined something to glorify Him, He will protect you so you have the chance to fulfill His plans for your life.

Today, I'm a certified drug counselor and have a bachelor's

degree in theology. Over the years, God has continued to sustain me even through difficult times. He helped me resist offers from old friends to get back into drugs. When I faced physical and mental challenges from HIV medication I take, God sent my brother-in-law and others to pray with me and see me through.

Back in 1984, doctors had given me two years to live, but sixteen years later I'm still alive. I continue to take medications for AIDS, but for more than four years, my doctors at the veterans hospital haven't detected the AIDS virus in my system during routine checkups. Am I healed of AIDS? Medically, that's thought of as impossible. But with God, all things are possible!

I no longer live with daily thoughts of dying but thoughts of life. I believe God allowed me to experience deep pain in my life in order to bring me the rewards He always intended for me to have. He was strengthening me and molding me to do His will—to counsel others who are faced with similar challenges.

When I accepted Christ into my life in the hospital, I realized the missing piece in my life was Jesus. Jesus took all the nonsense out of me—shooting heroin, cursing every other word—and He gave me the gift of counseling. Today when I help recovering addicts, I can give them more than book knowledge.

They usually ask me how I've stayed clean.

I ask them, "When you got out of detox, did it seem like something was missing in your life, a missing piece?"

They'd say yes and that's why they didn't know what else to do but go back to drugs. That's why they kept on relapsing.

"The missing piece is Jesus Christ," I tell them. "He's what's keeping me, and I'll never go back."

RONALD TYLER is a certified drug counselor and has a bachelor's degree in theology. He directs the HOPE ministry at his church, Greater Gethsemane Missionary Baptist Church, where he counsels members about AIDS. Tyler was appointed to serve as a member of the Veteran Affairs HIV Community Planning Board under former United States President Bill Clinton's administration. He resides in Baltimore with his wife, son, and twin stepdaughters.

THE VOICE OF GOD
Linda Watkins

Written by Linda Watkins

I was raised during the Civil Rights era. My parents were active in the movement in the North. My oldest sister was one of several children to integrate Teaneck, New Jersey's white elementary school in 1963. Two decades later, I graduated magna cum laude from an Ivy League university. I was one of Black America's children of promise.

In college I majored in African-American Studies and Organizational Behavior, but my passion since first grade was writing. Cocky, proud of my heritage, and politically active on campus, I saw myself as a young warrior who would help to change the world. There was no doubt in my mind that I would be successful. I had gone to college with sons and daughters of some of the wealthiest people in America. In addition, I was filled with a determination to better conditions for my people—Black people.

When a national business newspaper offered me a job as a staff reporter, I saw it as a golden opportunity. The newspaper assigned me to one of its small bureaus in midwest America. At the time, the city was the third largest corporate headquarters in the nation.

I was very excited about the job until I visited the newspaper's office and learned I would be its first full-time Black reporter. In 1984, more than twenty years after Dr. Martin Luther King Jr. delivered his famous "I Have A Dream" speech, I would be integrating this newspaper bureau. I was shocked but also believed that I was ready for the challenge.

I was no stranger to integration. From an early age, I understood the struggle and pain that accompanied it. When I was ten years old, my family moved from a predominantly Black neighborhood in Teaneck, New Jersey, to an all-white town in Andover, Massachusetts. My father, a systems manager at Volkswagen of America, had an opportunity to open his own car dealership. The move was traumatic, the most devastating experience in my life.

I went from being a popular and outgoing A student with friends of all nationalities in Teaneck to a social outcast and mediocre student among my peers and teachers in Andover. My new English teacher insisted I wasn't smart enough to be at my proper grade level. She pushed me back to the third grade. That made me feel so bad, like I was dumb. Only after my mother fought her decision was I moved back to fourth grade.

Both at school and in my new neighborhood, the only friends I had were my two older sisters. Even though I tried to make new friends, the other children simply wouldn't play with me. When teachers asked us to line up in pairs for school activities, I was always the child left without a partner. Those children who were forced to pair with me refused to hold my hand.

Many a day I cried after school and wondered why nobody liked me. Then I decided to create my own world with my own special friends. My best friends were my journal and the world of nature. I wrote in my journal every day and played in the woods behind my house for hours at a time.

After a year in Andover, my family moved to another white

town—Franklin, Massachusetts. The people there were predominantly Italian and much friendlier than those in Andover. Between the fourth and twelfth grades, I lived in Franklin and survived through a twofold strategy: fighting racism by excelling in academics, sports, and student leadership positions; and holding on to my Black culture for dear life.

Every chance I got, I returned to Teaneck to hang out with Black friends. I was also blessed to have an aunt who owned a Black bookstore in Harlem and periodically sent me books by Black authors. While my white peers in high school were having fun at keg parties, I was home reading *Roots, The Autobiography of Malcolm X, Soul on Ice,* and other Black classics.

During these years, I experienced racism but not to the extent I had in Andover. At school, I was treated by some students as an "honorary" white person. Because I was smart, outgoing, and talented, my race wasn't acknowledged at all! But when it came to dating, I was never asked out by a white guy. My senior-year guidance counselor also tried to discourage me from applying to top schools. He insisted that I try for a state school. Instead, I applied to Princeton and Brown Universities, as well as Wellesley College. I was accepted to all of them.

I chose Brown, and it was like an oasis after the desert experience of my adolescence. There I met other Black children of promise, some of whom also experienced racism and rejection growing up. In the midst of this Ivy League campus, I was part of a tight community of African-American, Latino, and Asian students who supported one another. I continued to excel academically and in student leadership positions. By the time I graduated, I felt like I could conquer the world.

So on my first day of work at my new newspaper job, I walked into a glitzy downtown skyscraper dressed to kill in a sharp business suit and cherry-wine briefcase. Although a bit nervous, I was still excited about the day. Then a building guard singled me out as I passed his desk in the midst of a crowd of white executives.

"Can I help you?" he asked in a tone that sounded accusatory.

"No. I work here," I responded with a stiff upper lip.

At first, I felt a sting of humiliation but then tried to give the older white man the benefit of the doubt. After all, I was a new face. Perhaps he was just trying to help.

I enjoyed meeting my new coworkers. They seemed cordial, and my bureau chief was almost fatherly. It was evident that I was the youngest person there and the least experienced in the field. But I was still determined to excel and work hard to write good stories that would talk about mainstream issues but also Black America.

By the next month, the novelty of the job had worn off. The coldness I felt from several coworkers made me feel alienated. I realized that outside of the newspaper, we had little to nothing in common. Still, I wasn't about to change who I was culturally to fit into their world.

I tried to be friendly toward my colleagues because I learned from my adolescent years that reaching out to white folk in a non-threatening way was the key to surviving in their world. I would participate in staff discussions about current events. But when I tried to initiate a conversation, I got a cold response. One day I asked several coworkers for their views on a major story that broke the day before; they showed little interest. Minutes later, the whole staff, minus me, gathered to talk about the topic I had raised! I was really angry but more hurt that they had intentionally excluded me.

The rejection I began to feel in my office was similar to my Andover experience. Racism also raised its ugly head out on the reporting field. One day I went to interview the chief executive officer of a major corporation. When I arrived at his office, I told his secretary who I was and the newspaper I represented. She informed her boss that I was waiting in the reception area. Ten minutes later, he poked his head out his office door, scanned the room, and acted like he didn't see me. I was the only person there, so I stood, introduced myself, and approached him.

"You're the newspaper reporter? You must have gone to a very good school," he said, dumbfounded. Yes, I had gone to a good school. But the point was I knew he had looked past me because I was Black.

On another assignment, a different executive refused to shake my hand. He just stared at me for several seconds, then pompously waved his hand as if to summon me to follow him into his office. I acted like I didn't understand. Only then did he audibly invite me into the room. It was a grown-up version of what I had faced when living in Andover when the white children at school wouldn't hold my hand.

These experiences were common, not exceptional. Regardless of my talent, hard work, and educational background, I sensed that many whites saw me as inferior because I was African-American.

The sting I had felt on my first day of work when the security guard singled me out had grown into a festering sore by early 1985. But instead of expressing my feelings and growing depression to family and friends, I convinced myself I just had to be stronger. My parents, friends, and former professors were so proud of me, and I had high expectations of myself. Freedom fighters of Black history—Harriet Tubman, Frederick Douglass, Ida B. Wells, Marcus Garvey and others—became role models of courage for me. Still I realized that none of my past experiences or books I'd read had prepared me for the racism I faced. I had tried to distance myself from the pain of racism by creating a wall around my heart, but my self-esteem was starting to crumble.

At the age of twenty-three, I wasn't even thinking about God as a source of support. I had been so bored at the Episcopal church my family attended when I was growing up that at this stage of my life, I was an agnostic who believed in a "supreme being," but that was about it. If I was going to overcome racism, it would be through my own intelligence, I thought.

I searched for other ways to calm my nerves, and liquor became a source of support. Every weekend I would hang out at a

Black club in town where young and middle-aged Black professionals drank, danced, and socialized. Many had also been recruited from other cities. Once bright-eyed and ambitious, many of us had become cynical.

Every day I would get angry because of the scarcity of African-Americans in my office building. Most were janitors and cooks; that added fuel to my fire. When I went out to cover corporate meetings, the first thing I did was scan the room for other Black people. Nine times out of ten, I was the only African-American there. In a city that was more than 25 percent Black, it was obvious that many Blacks had been kept out of corporate circles.

The more racism I saw and experienced, the more outraged I became. On the outside I may have looked normal. I was emotionally distant in order to appear strong. But each glare and stare from a white person felt like a stab in my heart. Even when my bureau chief gave constructive criticism on my work, I took it as a personal attack.

You see, racism is like poison. It has deadly consequences. Some may think it can't really harm you, but in sufficient doses it can kill. At first you may feel fine, then your perspective becomes blurred. Next thing you know, you're filled with rage. You may wear a mask that indicates everything is fine, but you're all torn up inside. With each new exposure to racism, a part of you dies.

My overdose came in February 1985 in the midst of a special reporting assignment. My bureau chief asked me to cover a business analysts' meeting in New York and handle an exclusive interview with the company's chief executive officer (CEO). I would fly to New York on his private plane and interview the CEO during the flight. For the first time in months I was excited.

The logistics for the trip were planned by telephone with the company's public relations officer. Finally, the day arrived when I would meet him and the CEO in person. The PR man picked me up at my apartment so we could briefly chat before the flight.

"You're the reporter?" he asked when I opened my door. He laughed nervously.

The ride to the airport was uncomfortably quiet. I sensed that something was wrong. When we got there, he conferred with his boss, then informed me that our plans had suddenly changed. I could ride to New York on the company plane, but the exclusive interview was off. When I asked the PR man for an advance copy of the speech, he told me it was no longer available. I boarded the plane with an entourage of seven white men in black business suits. There were no "hellos," not even an acknowledgement. No one spoke to me the entire plane ride.

That day I reached a point in my life where I began to question my existence. At the same time, I developed a hatred for all white people. While sitting silently on that suffocating plane, my mind raced through Black history. It began to replay the transatlantic slave trade, lynchings, and other atrocities against African-Americans.

The only thing that gave me strength was thinking about Harriet Tubman, one of the celebrated leaders of the Underground Railroad. She, too, must have felt alone at times, out on a limb in the middle of nowhere. But somehow she made it through, so maybe I could too. For a whole hour, I stored buckets of tears in secret compartments behind my eyes. I stared out the plane's window and pretended to dance on the clouds.

I left the group at the airport and hopped a cab to the analysts' meeting where I was the only Black person out of 100 people in the room. But this time I ignored the stares and concentrated on my mission: to secure and report the story before my newspaper's competition. I succeeded and went to my paper's headquarters, but the only person who greeted me there was a Puerto Rican intern. She helped me find a desk and a typewriter to use. She also let me know that a white female reporter had stolen my story off the news wire.

"She thought she was covering that meeting and was mad *you* were there," the intern said.

Racism? I wasn't sure, but it didn't make me feel any better, especially when I found out that I only had twenty minutes to write the story before the paper's deadline. Once again, the thought of Harriet Tubman helped me through that seemingly impossible task.

I was mentally, physically, and emotionally drained when I left the office that evening and boarded a 747 home. Within minutes I was asleep, and everything was fine until I woke up in a cold sweat somewhere over Maryland.

"I forgot to change that number in the story!"

That was real, not a dream. A financial error in the company's quarterly earnings would appear in tomorrow's first edition. I cried like a baby and tried to imagine my editor's disappointment and my colleagues' "I told you so."

The spirit of Harriet Tubman must have been helping someone else at that particular moment and two weeks later when I was bawling on my living room rug. Still grieving from discrimination I had faced during the New York trip and the correction in the newspaper, I was deep in navy blues and couldn't get out. I felt like I was having a nervous breakdown but was too proud to call someone for help.

As I sat there crying on my living room rug that night, I envisioned myself with a large machine gun. Any white person who got in my way would be executed on the spot. Horrified by my own thoughts, I turned the gun on myself.

"You're a failure, Linda. You don't deserve to live," a voice pounded in my head. *"You're inferior, Linda, and you'll never be accepted."*

I saw my car driving off a bridge into a river, then my body lynched, then my own hands stabbing me. *"Stab yourself, Linda! You deserve a gruesome death,"* the voice urged several times.

So I made my way to the kitchen in search of the stainless-steel knives I'd received as a Christmas gift. As soon as my foot hit linoleum, another voice intervened.

"Wrap the knives in newspaper and throw them on the porch,"

this calm, yet firm voice said. I'm not sure what made me listen to that voice, but I wrapped the knives in newspaper and did what it said.

Then I returned to my living room and fell to the floor. I was rolling back and forth violently, completely out of control. I had no idea what was happening, so I screamed.

"Help me! God have mercy on meeeeeeee!"

To this day I don't know why I cried out to God. Maybe deep down inside, I knew He was near. The room got absolutely quiet. I stopped rolling and dragged myself to a chair. As soon as I sat down I felt a warm, soothing force all around me, as if I were being hugged with giant invisible arms. I was sitting at a table with my typewriter and lit a thin white candle beside it. The light of the candle seemed to dance off the typewriter keys.

"God, is that You?" I asked, but there was no response. "If it's You, why'd You make me? I don't deserve to live." Again, no response.

Now I had no intention of moving my fingers onto the typewriter keys. It happened almost mechanically, and my fingers just started typing:

A POET.

A BLACK SCHOLAR.

A TEACHER OF BLACK HISTORY.

A FREELANCE WRITER.

I stared in disbelief. Then I consciously typed, LORD, IS THIS WHAT YOU WANT ME TO DO?

My fingers typed mechanically again. LINDA, IF YOU WANT IT TO BE SO, MAKE IT SO.

For the next hour, I received telephone calls from friends and family members across the country. A young man I had mentored in journalism called to thank me for the role I had played in his life. A friend from California called to say how much our friendship meant to him. My sister in Boston said she just felt compelled to call me and tell me she loved me.

God showed up that night and proved to me firsthand that He is real! I had heard the voice of God for myself, and it saved my life. That evening I also heard the devil. But God is more powerful than him. That's why I'm alive today.

God taught me that He is as close as the call of His name. No matter how low we've fallen or how depressed we are, He has the power to save our lives. Only God can heal the deepest wounds and scars in our souls, whether caused by racism or anything else that breaks our spirit. But we must be willing to humble ourselves, put our pride aside, and cry out to God for help from that deep place within.

My healing from wounds of racism didn't happen overnight. It has taken years for me to regain my self-esteem and confidence. The more I have walked with God and Jesus Christ, the greater my capacity has been to love all people and forgive those who are racist. God has taught me to have compassion for people who oppress others because of their own insecurities and fears.

As the prophecy God gave me for my life has unfolded over fifteen years, I've found that much of my life work has focused on racial reconciliation. Thanks to God, I am still a child of promise.

LINDA WATKINS is a professional writer and a consultant to nonprofit organizations. She began her writing career in 1984 as a journalist. She is a poet and playwright whose African-American history plays have been performed for young people and adults in Pennsylvania. In 1997, Ms. Watkins was called into the ministry of writing. *God Just Showed Up* is her first nonfiction book. She is a member of Covenant Church of Pittsburgh, a nondenominational multiracial church that models a racially reconciled world.

4
THE GOD WHO GUIDES OUR PATH

Have you ever wondered how Harriet Tubman did it? How could an ordinary Black woman flee from slavery, then return to the South to help 300 others escape? Not once. Not twice. Harriet made nineteen trips from the South to the North leading Underground Railroad passengers through woods, fields, and swamps. Our ancestors called her Moses because she led so many people out of slavery into freedom.

What's most striking is that Harriet never got caught, despite a large reward for her capture. She traveled mostly at night, guided by stars, though never trained in astronomy. Some scholars suggest Harriet's deep faith in God was the key to her success.

God continues to guide Christians through dangerous ground today. Whether career choices or life-threatening predicaments, the Lord is a headlight to all who follow Him.

[Jesus] said, "I am the light for the world!
Follow me, and you won't be walking in the dark.
You will have the light that gives life."

JOHN 8:12 (AJE)

BEYOND THE COMFORT ZONE
Chloe Coney

Written by Michele Drayton

When you're climbing up the corporate ladder, you seldom look back. By age thirty-three, I had reached the high rungs—high enough, perhaps, to barely glimpse the ground where I started.

My family lived in a spacious five-bedroom, three-bath house on two acres of land in Florida. We were particularly proud of the 700-series BMW in our garage and the fact that we were the first African-Americans to move into that bucolic suburban community. It was miles and worlds away from inner city Tampa, Florida, where I grew up. I was young, gifted, Black, and successful.

My husband and I gained entry into corporate America in the early 1970s when corporations were opening doors to talented Black college graduates. He was a production coordinator for an aerospace company. I was a marketing representative employed by a major utility corporation. Our two sons attended a private Christian school. They played Little League with the children of our white middle-class neighbors and friends.

This was the kind of life my grandmother, in particular, had wanted for me. A college graduate herself, she urged, "Chloe, go off to college and be somebody."

She had taught school for forty-five years, raised six children, and bought a house and a car. Her example fed my inner fire. She wanted me to carry a briefcase on my job. So in school I strove for the top of my class; in social circles, the life of the party.

Considering how far I'd come, I believed success began at bootstrap level, and I looked with indifference at others who hadn't begun to pull up theirs. I had made it out of the inner city, and if I could make it out so could anyone else, I thought.

I didn't even drive through my old neighborhood anymore. Truthfully, who would want to? I'd heard drugs had turned the inner city into a frightening place. Everybody was afraid to go back. Whizzing by on the highway in my sporty red Datsun, I felt no need to check out reports for myself. I was like many African-American professionals who left the inner city for the suburbs. I was in my middle-class orbit and perfectly content.

Spiritually, I also felt content. How could I look at my marriage, my house, and my job and not feel blessed by God? I had embraced Christianity at age twenty-six after straying from church during my fun-filled college days. As adults, both my husband and I had become faithful churchgoers. He even taught a Bible study in our neighborhood.

Bible Scriptures were part of my daily diet. Each morning, I'd listen to a Christian radio station as I drove to $300,000 homes in golf-course communities to sell my company's products. During lunch hour, I read the Bible. I diligently fed my spirit but within a comfortable sphere, all the time believing I was living according to the Lord's will. Nothing in my life suggested otherwise, until my late thirties when things began to change.

Emptiness welled up inside of me that material blessings no longer soothed. I didn't get a promotion after working for my company seven long years, including two years spent as a temporary employee. I began to ask the Lord hard questions: "Where am I going with my life? God, You saved me. You allowed me to have a lot of success. But what's next?"

Through prayer and Bible study, God nudged me to consider returning to school, but not for an M.B.A. or another prestigious degree. For some reason, God impressed on me the urge to study biblical counseling. "Counseling? People? That's me, anyway," I reasoned. Perhaps God wanted me to work in a church someday.

After inquiring, I found out a nearby Bible college had launched its first master's program and offered a concentration in biblical counseling. Still employed by the utility company, I began to take classes at night. Soon I would learn that entering the program was the first of several "divine appointments" steering me toward a new path in life.

One of my instructors, a Jewish man who became a Christian, stirred my inner unrest. He had a Ph.D. and the intellect to take him many places, but he chose ministry.

"God wanted more from me in my life," he told my class. Then he urged us to sift our motivation: "Do you really want to do the Lord's work? Would you be willing to make that sacrifice? Would you be willing to give up your salary, if necessary?"

I admired him for making the sacrifice, but I couldn't see myself doing it. I was glad someone else had gone into the ministry, but didn't know if that was my calling.

Under that instructor's guidance, I began to soul search. He taught that in order to help others, we had to identify our own priorities, values, and hang-ups. Poverty was clearly one of mine.

I was fifteen years old when my mother divorced her second husband and moved my younger sister and me into a public housing complex. At that time my mother made a living by cleaning other people's homes. "Don't mess up your life like I did. Go to college," she often told me. "That way you won't have to worry about anyone taking care of you."

Back then public housing didn't carry the stigma it does today.

The projects we lived in were actually in the same neighborhood as our old house. Because of segregation, ours was a predominantly Black community with a mix of residents from blue-collar workers and housewives to physicians and teachers.

Not until my later years in high school did I learn my family was poor. Part of the integration generation, I took a city bus to a mostly white school across town. The school was in a part of Tampa one would call elite. A lot of students there drove cars and lived in really nice homes. When asked where I lived, I'd simply say "West Tampa" to avoid being linked to the projects.

Throughout my high school years, I hid my address from classmates. It was hard enough having to justify my presence at the school. Some white peers couldn't fathom that I was an honors student because I'd come from schools they looked down upon. Others marveled that I—a Black girl—had attained leadership positions like vice president of student council. I must admit, graduating from that predominantly white school in 1968 was like a badge of honor for me.

As an adult, I hadn't resolved my unease with poverty or lingering scars of racism. I really didn't want to even be around poor folk.

But in reality, when I recall my past, there were more positives than negatives. I had excellent teachers and role models. Neighbors were kind and helped one another out. A group of African-American fathers in our area even raised money to buy a bus so the sports team from the Black high school wouldn't have to ride in hand-me-down buses.

The more I reflected, the more I asked, "What have I done to give back?" I began to wonder if God was pulling me in that direction—back home.

I began to spend Saturdays fulfilling internship requirements for my master's degree. I was assigned to a small church led by an Italian minister from New York. The church was near my old neighborhood and hardly rich, but I saw how God provided for this modest house of worship as members prepared food for needy people, including homeless men who lodged under a bridge.

As I scooped out potatoes one Saturday, someone called my name, "Chloe." The voice from the past came from a body I hardly recognized. Overweight and unkempt, she looked nothing like the slim, college-bound majorette I remembered. We had attended the Upward Bound program as high school students.

After she finished eating, I walked over and asked, "How are you doing?" My former classmate broke into tears.

"I'm on crack and feel hopeless, like there's no reason to go on," she cried.

Immediately, I took her hand and offered to pray. We prayed together, and I could tell she was moved.

"I need to get right with God, Chloe. Would you visit me sometime?" she asked.

The next week for the first time in about ten years, I exited the highway and drove down the main street leading to the projects. I had heard that my old neighborhood had deteriorated but was bowled over by the scene unfolding before me. Trash lay strewn on sidewalks once covered by grass. Music from boom boxes drowned out sounds of children's laughter. Young Black men hugging street corners waited for the next drug customer. Children ran about wildly with no apparent supervision.

The snapshots filed in my memory seemed like they were from a different world. I remembered clean porches, small gardens, and neighbors exchanging gossip and advice as they raked their front yards. I remembered friends who lived here packing suitcases for college. There were high expectations in the neighborhood when I was growing up.

As I entered my former classmate's apartment, my unblinking eyes panned the disarray. She had a son, but I noticed there was barely enough food in the refrigerator for a single meal. We talked about old times. She told me how her life had fallen like a house of cards. She wasn't alone.

131

"So many people we knew hit rock bottom," she told me. I could no longer contain my tears. We cried and prayed for them.

As I shut the door to leave her apartment, those nagging questions about my purpose were resolved. My purpose suddenly had a form and a face. God wanted me back here, to help people like my old classmate regain hope. It became crystal clear what my destiny in life was: God was telling me to come back and give to my community.

I wasn't sure how I would execute this, but that didn't stop me from telling my family and friends about it.

"God is calling me back to the inner city," I declared one day while eating lunch with several friends. They had climbed up the corporate ladder like me and wondered why I considered going back.

"Don't you remember how hard it was to get your job?" one friend warned. "You worked two years before you became a permanent employee. Jobs like that don't just come up." Still, I didn't budge.

I continued to chew on the idea and, as a result, had no trouble selecting a subject for my master's thesis at the Bible college: "Biblical Community Counseling Center in the Inner City of Tampa." I collected information from ministers of inner-city churches and from an African-American woman who managed a neighborhood service center in the heart of the projects.

In my research and personal study, I read about the biblical figure Nehemiah, the leader who returned to his Jerusalem birthplace to help the disgraced children of Israel rebuild the city's damaged walls. Like Jerusalem, the neighborhood around the projects had become a modern-day disgrace.

Nehemiah resurfaced in a speech I heard by an African-American Christian author. He had left his corporate job to return to his hometown in Mississippi. He went back not to lead but serve, by helping residents uncover their capacity to lead.

I incorporated everything I learned into my thesis, which discussed how a biblically based community center could restore the lifeblood of the inner city. It included mentoring programs for boys, programs to strengthen ties among neighbors, and parent alliances with schools.

But I also believed the community had its own resources to address many of its needs. My old neighborhood had "natural healers"—grandmothers who sat on porch steps and dispensed kernels of wisdom. It had churches that provided spiritual guidance and trained youngsters to read and speak in public.

In my thesis, I repeated some of the words shared with my friends: "I left the inner city without making an impact on the community for Jesus Christ. Now, I want to return to my old neighborhood and give something back, using the talents and gifts with which God has so richly blessed me."

I graduated from the Bible college in June 1989. The next month, the neighborhood service center manager whom I had interviewed for my thesis was killed in the center's parking lot. The woman's boyfriend shot her to death right at her place of employment. I worked with her cousin and learned about her death over lunch with colleagues. We all were saddened and shocked.

While touring Florida colleges with my son that summer, I ran into an old classmate from junior high school. Now a human resource manager, he worked for the county government. I told him I worked at a utility company but felt God was calling me back to inner-city Tampa.

"Do you know of any job openings?" I asked. He brought up the slain center manager and said the agency was searching for a new director. The job entailed coordinating a wide range of social services for low-income residents. Compared to my corporate position, it sounded like going from the White House to the outhouse. I was working with people whose household incomes were easily six figures. The neighborhood center job involved people on welfare who could barely pay their rent.

Still, I applied for the job. It seemed like all of the recent events in my life were pointing me in that direction: my thesis on an inner-city community counseling center, meeting the former manager of the neighborhood center and participating in an internship project near my old neighborhood.

When I told my mother, she thought I had flipped.

"Chloe, you fixin' to leave the power company to go work where?" she asked. "Don't you know that woman got killed in that parking lot? That's where the riots happened."

"You've got a good job," a friend warned. "You know how hard it is to find a good job. If you quit, there's no coming back."

Fortunately, my husband supported me wholeheartedly. He, too, had begun soul searching and wondered if he should rethink his career. The job change wouldn't affect our household salary dramatically. The biggest consideration was leaving corporate America. When you leave the business world, you lose the company car, the 401(k) program match, and other perks.

I almost didn't make the finalist cut for the manager's job because I lacked supervisory experience. But my former classmate, the one who mentioned the job, persuaded county officials to keep my application.

I'll never forget the day of the interview. I felt nervous until I opened my car door. I looked toward the sky, and it seemed to open up. It was brighter than any I'd seen. Then a Scripture suddenly came to mind from 2 Kings 6:16 (KJV): *"Fear not,"* the prophet Elisha told his servant. *"They that be with us are more than they that be with them."* God was telling me not to be afraid. Incredible peace rushed into my soul. I felt God's presence all around me.

I walked into the building to face a panel; some of its members were community advisory leaders who lived in the neighborhood.

"I'm mentally, emotionally, and spiritually ready for this job," I told them. "I'm coming back to Tampa to give back. This is my community—and I really want to give back. That's the reason I want this job." Within two weeks, I was hired.

Since that fall day in 1989, God has directed my work in Tampa's inner city. He even led me to start a community development corporation five years into my neighborhood center job. The Corporation to Develop Communities of Tampa is now a nonprofit organization with a $2 million budget. It is currently participating in an $8.5 million joint venture to build houses and apartments for local residents.

Among other things, the CDC runs a business incubator for African-American small business owners in the inner city, a full-scale coin laundry in walking distance of two projects, and a mentoring program for African-American boys. The organization has gained favor with funding agencies and wealthy executives.

But none of this has been easy. There were times when I wondered if the staff or light bills would be paid. There have been personal costs, too. My family left our five-bedroom house and moved to a smaller home. After an injury cost my younger son's football scholarship, he had to leave college until he raised more money for his tuition. We couldn't afford to pay it all. He's currently working to get back into school.

But through everything, God has brought us through. While I was living in the suburbs, residing in my comfort zone, I read about God and His goodness in the Bible. Now I know about His goodness because I've experienced God's blessings firsthand. Like Nehemiah, the Lord led me to help restore my broken community. Today the glitzy offices and fancy cars of my past cannot compare to the joy I get from helping an unemployed person find a job or seeing new hope in a child's eyes.

In a process that sometimes takes years, God rebuilds us in order to bring us face-to-face with His purpose for our lives. Often that process is uncomfortable, sometimes even painful, but the result is fulfillment.

In my natural mind, I could never have thought of half the services of the development corporation I oversee. God leads us each day in every way. We just have to listen and obey.

 **CHLOE CONEY** is president and chief executive officer of the Corporation to Develop Communities of Tampa. Married thirty years, she and her husband have two sons, a daughter, a daughter-in-law, and a granddaughter. The Coneys attend Mountaintop International Church in Tampa where she is an evangelist and her husband an associate pastor.

A NEW MAN THROUGH CHRIST

Lewis Lee

Written by Linda Watkins

I was fifteen years old when I entered prison. Today, I'm forty-one. I'm what you call a "lifer," a prisoner with a life sentence. Thanks to God, I'm not the same person I used to be. When I first came to prison, I was a young street thug—a cold-hearted robber, drug dealer, and user. But over the years, God changed me into a servant of the Lord.

My life of crime started when I was ten years old. That's when I first got involved in gang activity in Philadelphia. Even though my family was lower middle class and my parents tried to raise me the best they knew how, I chose not to listen to them. Instead, I hung out in the streets. I wasn't interested in school and didn't even think about the future back then. Instead, I lived for the day and getting high. Me and my friends smoked marijuana. If I was high every day, I was happy.

The first time I came in contact with the law was back in 1973, when I was thirteen. I was placed on probation for shoplifting. The next year, I was sent to two different juvenile institutions, both times for skipping school. The night of my second release, several friends taught me how to inject speed. At first, when I watched them sticking needles in their arms, I was like, "Wow! This is a little too deep for me." But a half hour later I tried it and liked how I felt.

From that point on, my life was one downward spiral. I began to rob and steal and do whatever I had to do to get money to get high. I didn't care about anybody but myself and was living to satisfy my needs.

The crime that led to my life sentence happened four months later. On March 25, 1975, one of my partners and I were hanging out in our neighborhood. We walked into a store and met a man who said he'd sell us his car at a cheap price.

"Let's go and rob something so we can get money for the car," I said. My partner, who was two years older than me, was down with the idea.

We'd been doing a lot of robberies for money and drugs, so we knew we could pull this thing off. He suggested that we rob a drugstore. We made fast arrangements and got several guns. That night, we drove from Philadelphia to Delaware County. Our goal was to stop at a drugstore and steal drugs and whatever cash was there. We were gonna sell some of the drugs to make more money and keep the rest for ourselves.

When we got to a drugstore my partner knew about, it was around 10:00 P.M. The store looked closed, so we left our car and headed toward the front door. Through the window, we could see two people inside. We decided to wait until they came out, figuring we could rob them, too. When the men left the store, they headed for a car, and as soon as they got inside, we ran toward them.

"Go toward the big guy on the passenger side," my partner said. He was gonna handle the guy on the driver's side.

Although I was only fifteen, I had no fear. I figured I'd pull out my gun and flash it so the man on the passenger side would cooperate. But instead, the big guy opened his door and pointed a bigger gun at me! I froze, then ran, and the guy started shooting after me. That's when fear set in. I remember hearing all these gunshots. I didn't know the area at all, so I just kept on running. I spotted a parking lot next to an apartment building and thought I'd be safe there. So that's where I hid for a while. But the next thing I knew, the sky was covered with helicopters. Along with the helicopters, there was a search party on foot looking for me, but I didn't know it at the time. Without thinking, I stepped out from where I was hiding, and someone from the search party saw me. I was caught, cuffed, and put into a police car.

I sat silently in the backseat as they drove me back to the drugstore. On the way, I overheard one cop say that someone had been killed. I hadn't known that because the only shots I was aware of were the ones fired at me. When we got to the drugstore, the big guy identified me.

"Yeah, he was one of them," he said.

It turned out the people we were trying to rob were police officers dressed in civilian clothes. My partner shot and killed one of them. The guy he killed, though, was more than a policeman. He happened to be the chief of police!

After the guy identified me, several cops drove me to a police station on a little street. I just knew they were going to kill me when we got inside. I was scared, you hear me. I was scared. There were no other people in the building, and the lights were real dim. They let their dog loose on me and physically abused me. But when it was all over, I was alive.

At the trial that followed, I didn't have a lawyer; I had a public defender. He advised me to plead guilty to second-degree murder; that's murder committed without premeditation but with some intent. I didn't know any better because I was so young, so I pleaded guilty to the charge. The judge went along with that and charged my partner with first-degree murder. We were handled like adults rather than juveniles and given life sentences.

In many ways, going to prison was like a homecoming for me because my older brother was there and so were friends from the streets. I quickly found that life in prison wasn't a whole lot different from the outside world. Although I was behind bars, I could still get drugs, get high, and gamble. My brother and partners watched my back just like they did out in the streets, but in prison they protected me from rape and other kinds of violence. They helped me transition into prison life. That was important because I was only fifteen and totally surrounded by grown men.

After several months, prison life began to feel natural to me. I wasn't even bitter at the public defender who sold me out by telling me to plead guilty. But back then I didn't fully understand my jail sentence. I had no idea I'd be in prison literally for the rest of my life.

Several inmates told me about a lifers' organization made up of guys with life sentences. I got involved with the group, and the men got me thinking about things other than getting high. They talked about the importance of education, so I started going to school in prison and got my GED. Eventually, I started taking college classes through a special program at Harrisburg Area Community College. The prison program allowed me to work toward an associate's degree in business management.

The lifers also got me thinking beyond myself. We did special projects like selling cards and hoagies to inmates. When we made money from activities, we'd use the cash to buy law books, fix up things for inmates, and give money to charities. But that was the good side of me. There was also a whole lot of bad. You can take a kid out of the streets, but it's harder to take the streets out of a kid.

I was doing drugs constantly and getting thrown in the hole for that and other prison infractions. The hole is like solitary confinement. It's a very depressing place because you're locked in a cell twenty-three hours a day with no human contact. The only time you're allowed out of your cell is for one hour during the day, and that's strictly to exercise and shower. What drives a lot of guys crazy is there's nothing to do in the hole, and each cell faces a brick wall. Prisoners in the hole shouted at the top of their lungs to try to communicate with one another. We even came up with our own chess game that worked by calling out moves according to numbers. We also held mock trials for new guys coming into the hole. Anything to keep our minds occupied for the ten, twenty, and thirty days we were there.

When I got out, I continued to do drugs and fight. I was also involved in homosexuality. I was a very sexually active teenager at the time I entered prison. When I saw men there acting and wanting to be treated as women, I knew homosexuality was an avenue to satisfy my physical needs. I never would have done that outside of prison, but there were no women around, so I adapted to my new world.

Needless to say, at that stage of my life, God was the farthest thing from my mind. I knew there was a God, but He was in His world, and I was in mine. That was the way things had been with God and me all of my life. I only went to church a couple of times as a child.

The only thing that got me thinking about God in prison was a girl. She was the sister of one of my friends from the neighborhood. She would come to visit me, and we'd talk and laugh. Soon I learned that she was a Christian, but she wasn't heavy into the church thing. In time, I fell in love with her and noticed she was getting more serious about following God. I knew that if I was gonna keep her in my life, I'd have to get to know the God she knew.

One day she started talking to me about Jesus Christ. It was the first time I'd ever heard about Him.

"He's a man who died for your sins," my girlfriend said. I believed her just out of not knowing anyone else who'd ever done that—dying for somebody else's sins.

Several nights later, in 1983, I got on my knees in my cell and asked Jesus to come into my life. I was motivated more by wanting to keep my girlfriend than feeling the need for a personal savior. But I still noticed a change in me after that night. For the first time in my life, I wanted to live right.

I'd heard about the prison church, and that was one of the first places I went the next day. Soon afterward, my girlfriend sent me a Bible, and I picked it up at the chapel. The chaplain handed me my Bible and said, "Here, have a good day." That was it. There was no love, no joy, no nothing. I was really disappointed but still determined to get to know God because I was serious about keeping my girlfriend.

I started reading the Bible and praying in my cell, and going to the prison church on Sundays. Before long, I stopped desiring drugs, homosexual partners, and gambling. It was something to see the change in me, but I also felt alone. I didn't have any close friends in prison who were Christians, and a lot of the guys at the church seemed cold. Three months into my new lifestyle, someone offered me a stick of reefer. I took it, smoked it, and was back on drugs again.

Looking back, I think I returned to my old lifestyle because, despite the things I was doing right, I didn't have a personal relationship with the Lord. I was motivated by keeping my girlfriend and didn't have a lot of other support at the prison. Somebody has to nurture you when you're a baby in the faith, or the devil will snatch you and steer you toward your old ways.

That's what happened to me. The next six years of my life were like a roller-coaster ride, mostly downhill. I started doing all the bad things I did before I asked the Lord to come into my life: using drugs, selling narcotics, gambling, and having sex with men. Of course, I also lost my girlfriend.

I had a total of eighteen misconducts on my prison record, and most of them happened during this six-year period. There was suspicion of sodomy, possession of drugs, possession of money, possession of materials to manufacture fermented beverages, possession of a weapon, and fighting. My time in the hole forced me to drop out of the college classes I was taking. Then the government aid program that funded the classes was cut, so I couldn't finish my degree requirements.

My destructive lifestyle continued all the way up until 1989. That was the year I felt the Lord convicting my heart. All of a sudden, I started feeling guilty every time I did something bad. Now I don't know why it happened that year. All I know is that I felt sorrow in my heart, and that feeling of sorrow and the tugging in my heart were real. I started getting sick of my lifestyle—the drugs, fighting, foul language, and homosexuality. For the first time, I saw that my life was going around in a circle, just like one of the TV commercials talked about. You see this man in a little room and he's walking around. "I do more coke so I can make more money. I make more money so I can do more coke," he says. It was clear he wasn't going anywhere. It was clear the guy was stuck.

That's basically what my life was like at the time. I was just going 'round and 'round in a circle. If I could be high all day, then it was a wonderful day. I had the same mentality that I had when I was fifteen and a kid on the streets.

With that realization, I started hearing God whisper to me, "There's a better life for you." It was like God was calling me back to Him, telling me to follow Him because I wasn't getting anywhere on my own. But I still didn't act on that. As sick as I was of my lifestyle, I wasn't ready to give it up. It took several more months for me to commit to change.

What prompted that was a major riot at my prison in October 1989. Tension was mounting because of severe overcrowding in the prison, the removal of some programs and services for inmates, as well as general unrest. You know, when you have dynamite sitting close to fire, you can't control the explosion. Well, one day the prison exploded. Frustrated inmates set fire to buildings and tore up property. Prison guards were taken as hostages, and the prison grounds were like a war zone. In the end, fourteen buildings were destroyed and more than a hundred people injured. Amazingly, nobody died during the two nights of rioting. Police came in and eventually took back the prison, but a whole lot of damage had been done.

During the whole thing, I know that God was watching over me because I didn't get involved in the rioting. If I had, it would have caused a lot of problems for me afterward.

After the riot, a lot of changes happened at the prison. Guys were locked down, four men to a cell, cuffed and shackled in leg irons. Some of those cells were intended for one man but ended up with four because of damaged cell blocks. The prison started transferring hundreds of inmates to other prisons across the country. Everyone was on edge; as a result, the prison got real quiet. Nobody was talking. Everybody was just waiting to see what was gonna happen. I know it was only by the grace of God that I didn't get transferred out. I think God kept me there because it was my time to come back to Him. If I had left and gone to some other state, I wouldn't have been able to hear God because of all the changes in my life.

During this time of intense solitude, I heard God's voice repeatedly. "Come back to Me," He was saying. But I still wasn't ready.

At the time, I was in a cell with three other men who eventually got transferred out. That left me in a cell by myself. Then I learned that I'd be getting a cell mate. I was thinking, *Wow, I might get lucky and they might bring a homosexual into my cell.*

But lo and behold, the guy they brought in was a Christian. The twenty-year-old had entered prison a few days before the riot and was serving a five- to ten-year sentence for selling drugs. Apparently, during his first few weeks in jail he accepted Jesus as Lord. So he was young in the faith. At the time, I was thirty years old. Wow, was I disappointed that this young Christian guy was my new cell mate. I knew his arrival was a sign from the Lord. God was saying again, "It's time to recommit your life to Me."

I started thinking about all the times when God had looked out for me. He saved my life as a kid on the streets when I could have and should have been dead from gang violence. He protected me from being raped and overdosing on drugs in prison. Now God was sending me a Christian cell mate instead of a homosexual. Once again I heard Him say, "There's a better future for you, a better life ahead."

That's what made me get down on my knees again in early 1990 and surrender my life to the Lord, this time for my own good rather than for a girlfriend. I don't recall my exact words, but I remember meaning every word I said. I wanted to turn away from my old life and start a new life with God as my guide. To this day, my favorite Scripture is 2 Corinthians 5:17. It says, *"Therefore, if anyone is in Christ, he is a new creation; old things have passed away; behold, all things have become new"* (NKJV).

For the past ten years, I've looked to the Lord, and He has given me a new life. Almost immediately after surrendering my heart to Him in 1990, I no longer had the desire to use drugs, sell them, gamble, and swear. My heart had been changed. I didn't want the things I craved in the past. However, a couple of things just wouldn't go away, like the desire for cigarettes and sex with men. Then, the more I read the Bible and prayed, the more I was able to resist the temptation to do those things. Also, the more I tried to follow God, the more I started caring about other people and wanting to help them.

Now I didn't ask God to make me one of His servants. It just sort of happened. I started having a strong appetite for the Bible and began to memorize Scriptures. Then I joined a Bible study class and had a chance to usher in the prison church. Next I was reading Scriptures during services and eventually teaching Bible studies. That's how my ministry began.

I feel God's presence and peace in my life so strongly that I want other people to feel the same thing. I've discovered firsthand that if you don't know the Lord, you will never have peace in your life. You may think drugs, money, and power will bring you peace, but peace comes from knowing God. When you know God, you also feel His love and want to pass it on to others. God loves everybody, including prisoners who've done the worst crimes. He's calling all of us to confess our sins, turn away from them, and become new men and women who follow Him.

My prayer is that one day I'll be pardoned for my crime and leave this prison. If that happens, I want to minister to juveniles who are on the road to destruction like I was. I also want to do prison ministry and become a chaplain at a prison because I know the needs of inmates. In the meantime, I'm at peace even as a man who doesn't know when he's going home. What I know is when I die I'll be with the Lord, and heaven will be my home. For now I'm just a traveler on earth passing through life with God as my guide. But my mission here is clear: to lead others to the Lord.

 **LEWIS LEE** is a prisoner at the Pennsylvania State Correctional Institution Mahanoy in Frackville, Pennsylvania. He is serving a life sentence for being an accomplice in a robbery and murder when he was fifteen years old. Lee has spent more than twenty-six years behind bars. His only hope for release is to have his sentence commuted by the Governor of Pennsylvania. While in prison, Lee accepted Jesus Christ as his Lord and Savior. Today, he is a Bible study instructor for inmates on his block, an area comprised of sixty-four cells and approximately 120 prisoners. In addition, he helps run church services at the prison. If freed, he desires to become a prison chaplain and a minister to juveniles heading down the wrong path.

THE ACCIDENT

George W. Russell Jr.

Written by Linda Watkins

Growing up, church folks used to say, "The Lord is our strong tower."[1] To me, that always meant God's a source of strength. Not until the night of a near-fatal accident did I grasp the full meaning of the phrase.

Up to that point, my life was relatively carefree. I'd grown up with loving parents and always gotten what I needed. My folks weren't rich, by any means. But because of my ability to play music well, I started making money at a young age. At fifteen, I taught piano. By sixteen, I was gigging in nightclubs. Ever heard the expression "a self-made man"? Well, that's what I was.

Back then I took a lot for granted, even God. Although I'd grown up in church and went to service regularly, I never really understood the extent of God's power until the night of the accident.

It was a typical evening in late September my last year at Duquesne University in Pittsburgh. Part of my daily routine was to eat dinner around six, then ride to the university to teach a private piano lesson.

Did I tell you that I was a music education major? My career was all mapped out. I wanted to teach in a public school, play music around town, and raise a family. Back then, young Black men could pretty much write their ticket in the field of education. Since so few of us were teaching, I probably could have landed a job anywhere. But those plans changed after the accident.

I'd just left Kentucky Fried Chicken where I devoured some fried chicken, mashed potatoes, and cole slaw. Then I hopped on my motorcycle and headed north toward the university. It was really no big deal. I'd traveled that route many times before. Of course, I had no idea things would be different that night.

I was cruising toward the small bridge on the city's infamous Boulevard of the Allies. As usual, cars were traveling up two northbound lanes as I glided down a southbound corridor. Suddenly something unusual caught my eye: a car and a small pickup truck heading north on the boulevard. In a reckless test of egos, at the tail end of rush hour, the two drivers were trying to pass each other.

I bet it started as a simple game. First, the car successfully passed the truck. Then the truck tried to pass the car. But the truck driver's timing was off, and they collided.

Booom!

The truck driver lost control and the pickup jumped into my southbound lane. Without warning, more than 3,000 pounds of metal raced toward me. There was no time to think. No time to act.

Baaam!

That was all I remember hearing. Then silence. Blissful silence.

Have you ever flown before? I'm not talking about a plane ride. Just you and your body soaring through the atmosphere? Well, there I was flying into what seemed like another world. My whole body spun in midair. Funny thing was there was no noise. All I heard was a faint *sswwiiisshhh*. And that was air gushing through my helmet.

Amazingly, I was conscious the whole time. I remember flying for what seemed like eternity. Actually, about fifty feet passed before I hit the pavement. Then I bounced several times into a cement wall at the edge of the bridge.

Looking back, I know God carried me to the spot where I landed. If I'd flown another five feet, I would have plunged over the wall, dropping twenty-two feet into traffic below. And if I'd stopped sooner, I'd have crashed into oncoming traffic on the main boulevard.

God spared my life! I was blown away by that. He protected me and guided me in a miraculous way. That's not all; other blessings followed.

"I got hit!" I said to myself after landing. Then I screamed, *"Heelllppp! Heelllppp!"*

But nobody came to my rescue. So I cried out gently with the energy left, "Jesus, Jesus, Jesus, Jesus."

Suddenly time slowed down. I mean everything began to move in slow motion. Even my heart rate dropped. It was like I was in the twilight zone. Then out of the blue, God answered my prayer. Someone showed up. It was an off-duty police officer who had witnessed the whole accident. By the time he got to me, he'd already recorded the license plates and phone numbers of the car and truck drivers. He had also called an ambulance, which was on the way. All this within two minutes of crying out "Jesus"!

"What's your name?" the guy asked, genuinely concerned.

"George Russell," I answered, totally coherent.

"I need your license and wallet, George, so I can take care of things."

I pointed to my jacket pocket, and he gently lifted out my wallet. Around that time, I began to feel an excruciating pain in my left leg. It was the same sensation I felt while soaring through the air. That leg felt like it was way behind me. Now on the ground, I could see it was bent at a ninety-degree angle—not at the knee, but across my thigh. The whole leg was visibly swollen and throbbing through my pants.

When the ambulance arrived, a medic took off my left shoe. My foot swelled to five times its normal size. I couldn't believe what I was seeing. It was like a cartoon scene. Obviously, I didn't know the extent of my injuries. But rather than fear, I felt a strange sense of security. Ever since I called out "Jesus."

Minutes later, after being rushed to a major medical facility that happened to be right down the street, I learned my femur bone was completely broken in half. My left foot and toes were broken in several places, and hairline fractures lined my tibia, the thick inner bone in the lower leg. But outside of that, there were no other internal injuries! My mind was clear. Most important, there wasn't even a scratch on my piano-playing hands.

Amazing, powerful, mind-blowing! I thought.

How else could you explain something like that. I'm telling you, I was blown away. During my eighteen days in the hospital, I actually used to cry myself to sleep at night because I realized God's awesomeness for the first time in my life. I had seen the hand of God protect me and couldn't believe He loved me that much. But His blessings didn't stop there.

You see, all that time in a hospital bed gave me a chance to think. I saw how unsatisfied I was with my development as a musician. So I put my teaching plans on hold, applied to one of the most prestigious music schools in the world, and actually got accepted to the New England Conservatory of Music!

Since graduating from the conservatory, the Lord has blessed my music career. I've played all over the United States, participated in the International Jazz Piano Competition in Paris, and taught more than two thousand students through college courses and public school workshops. In 1991, I also became the minister of music at a church in Boston where I coordinate and play music at worship services and direct an arts ministry.

Looking back, my encounter with the Lord taught me God is real. This revelation came at a critical time and altered the course of my life. Often it takes tragic situations to make us see how great

God is and just how much we need Him. Every now and then, the Lord has to jolt us to help us understand how big and bad He is. Otherwise, it's so easy to go through life thinking we're in control, when all the time God's at the steering wheel. After all, "the Lord is our strong tower." He's protection in danger, a guide when lost, and strength when we can't go on. Twenty-four/seven, God knows what's going on. Simply put, He's the Man!

 **GEORGE W. RUSSELL JR.** is a professor at the New England Conservatory of Music's Extension Division. He is past chairperson of the division's Jazz Department. The pianist/composer is also on the faculty of Tufts University. He is the minister of music at New Covenant Church in Boston. A resident of that city, Russell has recorded five compact discs: *Communion, Communion Volume II, Jesus Is the Cure, Playing Praise,* and *Worship in the Style of G.*

---

1. See Psalm 61:3.

5
THE GOD OF SECOND CHANCES

Once upon a time there was a young man, the son of a wealthy father. He lived the "good life" but still wasn't satisfied. So he asked his dad for his inheritance, packed it in a four-wheel drive, and set out to discover the world. The son lived large at casinos, parties, and clubs until several months later his cash ran dry. Homeless and broke, the only job he could find was serving burgers at a fast-food restaurant.

It was there, at rock bottom, that the young man came to his senses. "My dad is rich. Home's where I belong. I need to go there and tell him I was wrong." The son was stunned when his father greeted him with open arms. The old man even threw a welcome-home party.

Like the Prodigal Son, God forgives us when we admit our wrongs, turn away from them, and choose to follow Him. He loves us so much, He allows us to start over again whether we've committed a crime or strayed from church or His divine plan for our lives. The stories in this chapter show that He is the God of second chances.

> *If we confess our sins, He is faithful*
> *and just to forgive us our sins and*
> *to cleanse us from all unrighteousness.*

1 JOHN 1:9 (NKJV)

RESISTING GOD

Dr. Mary Reed

Written by Linda Watkins

After four years of college, four years of medical school, and three years of special training in internal medicine, how could God possibly ask me to become a minister?

After all, I'm a woman. Women aren't supposed to preach, I thought. At least that's what I heard growing up in a strict church in Memphis. Its conservative leaders taught, "Women shouldn't lead in the church." And women teaching men in public was definitely out.

Besides, my new husband and I had mapped out the next five years of our lives. Becoming a minister was not in the picture.

So an episode in May 1983 caught me by surprise. The incident happened at my church in Detroit. At the time, I was finishing my medical residency at a hospital there. Like most Sunday mornings, by eleven o'clock the church was full. More than five hundred people lined the wooden pews with comfortable cushions. My pastor and his associates sat in the raised pulpit at the front while the choir sat majestically in a special section to their left. All was normal until Pastor shifted gears after an eloquent sermon.

"God has His hands upon a young lady in our church," he announced. "There's a special call on her life, a call to ministry."

Oh, that's wonderful, I thought turning around to see who he was talking about.

"I'm talking about Sister Mary Reed."

"What!"

Becoming a minister had never crossed my mind. Matter of fact, in two weeks I'd be moving to New York to start my medical career. Needless to say, when I arrived, my pastor's words were history.

The first month in New York went smoothly. I found a reasonably priced apartment, settled into my job, and waited for my husband to join me any day. But something equally exciting happened. I began to hear God's voice—clearly.

One night I was praying on my knees before bed. I started going through my regular list of prayers.

"Get up, Mary! Open your Bible and go to the book of Isaiah," I heard. *"Read Isaiah fifty, verses one to eleven."*

God's voice was so distinct, so clear in my mind. Obediently, I turned to the verses and began reading.

"The Lord God has given Me the tongue of the learned, that I should know how to speak a word in season to him who is weary . . ." (v. 4 NKJV).

That verse—verse four—practically jumped off the page.

"What's this?"

"I'm putting you on assignment," God answered.

"Me?" *He must be mistaken,* I thought. "If You want me to go into ministry, You're going to have to prove it."

So there. I went on with life and my medical career. Professionally, I was soaring. My job was going great. But my husband's job transfer was postponed. He wouldn't be able to join me in New York for several months. Until then, I was alone.

During that period, I tried to put God's words behind me, but He kept sending reminders. Like the time I was on the subway and several people asked if I was a preacher! I had on jeans and sneakers. No cross, Bible, nothing like that. There wasn't anything about me to prompt that question.

Then I started feeling a tugging inside. It was clear God wanted me to make a commitment.

"I'm already in Your ministry," I told Him one day. "Remember how I sang in a church choir during my medical residency? And I'm obviously in the ministry of healing people. I'm a doctor.

"But preaching? No way! Women don't preach. And we certainly don't lead men in church. We're supposed to be in the background."

Obviously God wasn't convinced. Shortly afterward, Sunday worship services changed. They used to be a refueling station, a source of inspiration, a place to get deeper insight. But now I couldn't get through a service with a dry eye. I kept on thinking about God's incredible love and how so many people didn't even know Him. Throughout church, tears would stream down my face. My heart was literally wrenched.

One night, on my knees, I budged a bit by asking the Lord for clarity on the preaching ministry. Out of the blue, an undeniable presence filled my bedroom. As sure as your breath, it was God.

"Mary, read Matthew nine, verses thirty-seven and thirty-eight."

I opened the Bible, and there it said: "*The harvest truly is plentiful, but the laborers are few. Therefore pray the Lord of the harvest to send out laborers into His harvest*" (NKJV).

"Mary, I'm calling you to be a laborer."

If I had any doubt about God's words that night, He took it away come Sunday. I was shocked when my new pastor opened his sermon with: "*The harvest truly is plentiful, but the laborers are few . . . .*"

Something inside of me broke when I heard those words again. Immediately, I walked to the altar at the front of the church.

"Why are you here?" a minister asked.

"I feel a calling on my life and want to acknowledge Jesus as Savior, King of my life."

Now that was progress. But I still wasn't ready to announce my call to the ministry. Before going public, I needed more signs. Not one. Many more.

"Lord, I guess You'll have to knock me in the head to confirm Your call," I said, laughing.

Several days later the joke was on me. I was in my kitchen preparing to fix a cup of tea. After opening a wooden cabinet to find tea bags, a bottle of olive oil suddenly fell off the top shelf. The bottle hit my hairline, then a light sprinkling wet my forehead. It ran down the front of my face.

When I went to wipe the oil off my shirt, my clothes weren't soiled. The oil had literally vanished. There weren't even traces on the counter.

"What's happening?"

There was silence. Then God's presence filled my kitchen. I felt an incredible sensation of peace, love, and lightness around me.

"I'm with you, Mary," the Lord said gently.

My God! Another sign. The Lord hit me in the head to confirm my call to ministry, just as I requested. He also anointed me. That means to put oil on you, to mark you for His service. How else could I explain how the cap screwed off the olive oil and how the glass bottle didn't crack after hitting my tile countertop?

"OK, God, I hear you. But I'm still a doctor, not a minister," I pleaded. I knew my mother could suffer if I became a preacher. Her church would surely put her out if folks found out her daughter preached like a man!

So for weeks I didn't tell anyone about the olive oil incident. Instead, I asked God for even more signs.

"Lord, if You want me in ministry, someone experienced in the church will have to confirm it."

Two months passed. My focus turned to job, family, and church. My husband was now in New York, and we became involved in an effort to support our new pastor. He was planning to run as a delegate for a presidential candidate. One Saturday morning, ten of his supporters met to strategize. We were in a church office when Pastor made an unexpected appearance.

"Good morning, everyone," he said, casually strolling into the room. Then as quickly as he came, he turned around and headed toward the door. Before he was totally out of sight, Pastor glanced back.

"Good morning, Reverend Dr. Reed."

He stared me right in the face. And so did everyone else after he said it. You see, my husband and I were new church members. I hadn't told anyone about my call to ministry, especially my pastor. His words were another sign and left me stunned.

Why was God pushing so hard, I wondered. Didn't He realize I couldn't go into ministry! That would mean I'd have to change my career path after I'd worked so hard to be a doctor. In fact, I never wanted to be anything else. When I was nine years old, my nightgown caught fire and burned more than ninety percent of my body. Most people thought I would die. But God allowed me to live. From then on, I knew I'd be a doctor and dedicate my life to helping people. That became my goal, and I didn't want to change it.

Accepting a call to ministry meant I'd have to give up that dream and control over my life. Ministry—not medicine—would have to be the priority. I just wasn't ready for that. I couldn't fathom it. So I continued resisting God and demanded extraordinary signs. I can still remember my last challenge.

"Lord, before I go public with my call to ministry, You'll have to knock me off my seat."

Lo and behold, a month later I was at a spiritual retreat. Six hundred women and men had flocked to a convention room in New York to hear a well-known evangelist. The room was crowded but remarkably peaceful when the dynamic preaching woman walked to the podium. All eyes were fixed on her as she shared a word from God.

The preacher talked about coming into the presence of the Lord. She talked about the importance of serving Him. Everyone focused intently on the evangelist's message until she abruptly stopped preaching.

"Someone in this room has a call on their life. I want you to stand up right now," she shouted into the crowd. "You hear me? Right now. Come on up here."

Her words were so jolting, I almost fell out of my seat! Luckily, I was able to grab the edge of the chair to avoid landing on the floor. I pushed my body up and managed to stand. But instead of walking to the stage, I ran out of the room! Thankfully, I was able to hide in a nearby bathroom. There, in a strange lavatory, I finally surrendered to God. The next Sunday, I voluntarily walked to the front of my church and announced my call to the ministry.

Today, I'm an ordained minister. I teach new members, lead a prayer group, and occasionally preach at my church. I'm also a full-time doctor and chief of oncology at a hospital. Can you believe after all I went through, the Lord allowed me to have two careers?

When I look back at all those months of resisting God, I can't believe how hardheaded I was. If only more of us realized how much God loves us! If only we understood He controls our lives! That year I learned that when the Lord orders our steps, there's really no turning back. It may take weeks or years to get where God wants us to be. But ultimately, as we yield, His plans are accomplished.

Thank You, Lord, for Your mercy and patience. Thank You for being the God of second chances.

 **DR. MARY REED** is chief of oncology at Bronx-Lebanon Hospital Center in the South Bronx community of New York City. She also serves as a cancer-liaison physician there. In 1998 and 1999, *New York* magazine listed her as one of the city's best medical oncologists. In addition to these responsibilities, Dr. Reed is an associate minister at Allen A.M.E. Church in Jamaica, New York, as well as an itinerant deacon in the general A.M.E. Church. She lives in New York with her husband and three children.

GOD'S GYM
Gary Shields

Written by Michele Drayton and Sheldon Ingram

My job is to get people in shape, the best shape they've ever been in. I pull out the greatness in people at my business, God's Gym. When I first opened my business, we were smack in the middle of the hood in West Oakland, California. Today we're located in downtown Oakland, but everybody still comes to God's Gym—prostitutes, drug dealers, cats coming straight from prison, lawyers, doctors, and others.

Some come to lift weights, others for spiritual food. Others because they can be themselves, and it's a great place to work out. A few used to be my running buddies back in the days when I was hustling to make ends meet. But God gave me a second chance at life, and that's my goal—to do the same for others.

At God's Gym, racism and other "isms" of the world don't exist. When people walk in, they feel warm and accepted. God's Gym is a bridge between the "haves" and "have nots." We call one another brother and sister, and everybody feels protected.

Here's the story of my life from a hustler to owner of God's Gym.

I'm a brother who didn't have to go to the streets and hustle —but did anyway. As a kid, my father worked as an aircraft mechanic and my mother as a nurse. After buying his first home and my mother having me, my father was laid off because of cutbacks. It was then that he decided he would never work for anyone again. With this decision and a lot of determination, my parents decided to launch their own business, a nursing home. My mother—a praying woman—said the Lord had told her the business would be a success. With their around-the-clock work, they made it one.

Within seven years, the business was making a lot of money. It was then that they decided to move to a nice home on an integrated block with Indians, Jews, Asians, and another Black family in El Cerrito Hill. A lot of the parents of the kids at the school I went to worked at my parents' business. Things were cool on my block, but on my way to school, I was having a hard time. White kids called me "nigger," threw eggs at me, and picked fights. Black kids also gave me the cold shoulder 'cause they assumed I thought I was better.

My parents were also having problems, but it didn't seem to bother my mother. In her thoughts it all was a game that she was winning, even when white people called her "girl" at her own nursing home. And my father was so good at business, that by the age of thirty, his net worth was more than a million dollars.

But at the age of twelve, I didn't understand any of this. I just sensed that everyone was playing a game. School continued to be a battle zone, and I had no real friends.

It was then that I joined a boxing gym in a tough neighborhood in West Oakland. I started hanging out at the gym so I could learn how to fight. My reasoning was that I wouldn't have to worry about people making fun of my speech problems or learning disabilities if I learned how to fight. I'd be like my idol, Muhammad Ali, who said no to Uncle Sam and his war. I'd be like the people who got the most respect in that neighborhood, the people who knew how to knock people out.

The gym taught more than fighting; the neighborhood introduced me to a world where cats ran numbers, collected women, and gambled. They kept their appearances up with nice jewelry and cars provided by rich white ladies. They focused on making money, just like my parents. They were businessmen whom I could relate to, and they made the rules in their own world.

The people who embraced me weren't the people who I went to school with. The so-called smart kids tried to make me feel dumb. It was the hustlers who took me in, and when I was down, their reply was, "Don't trip. We'll show you what smart is and how to make money."

These cats would stroke the wealthy women who came to the gym and would climb behind the wheel of BMWs and other fancy cars. In my mind, the women—mostly white and older—found those cats necessary, perhaps to validate that they weren't racist or that they were still attractive. I decided that if everyone's playing a game and getting paid for it, so would I. A known prostitute who often came by the gym taught me everything I needed to know about comforting high-class women—how to listen, when to compliment, where to rub. It was all about validating them—doing everything their husbands didn't.

So at fifteen years old, I became an "escort" to women two and three times my age. I'd meet them at the gym, and I soon had a steady clientele. The more women I stroked, the more money I stuffed into my pockets. I learned how to turn off my feelings when I was with them. The only thing I felt was my pocket full of money. You see, in the game, feeling has nothing to do with making money. That was my law.

Like any hustler looking for his next gig, I got involved in new areas: gambling and booking [illegal] numbers. I tried dealing crack—for a minute, but dropped it after a partner smoked the merchandise—an eight ball valued at $335. In a situation like that, you're supposed to make an example of that person. But that was never my thing, hurting people, unless they tried to hurt me. So I left that hustle alone.

All the while, I kept up my clean image as high school graduation approached by working at my parents' nursing home, a lumberyard, clothing stores, and other places.

In the early 1980s when I was nearly eighteen, I left home. My father persuaded me to enroll in a business college by paying half my rent. But school didn't last long; I dropped out because I knew the courses that I was taking wouldn't put money in my pocket.

My girlfriend—a fine young lady I had met in my grandmother's church on Easter—had moved in with me after her mother kicked her out. She acted kind of rough sometimes, but always had my back. After being together for a few years, we were, as much as I knew love to be, in love. Still, we'd fight like crazy, then make up. I didn't know any other way; this was how I'd heard and seen love.

Although our relationship was painful, my girlfriend wasn't the only source of my pain. Every couple of months, I would buy a bottle of wine—I didn't even like the stuff—and get sloppy drunk and curse myself out and cry. I'd stare into a mirror—and *bam!* I remembered myself as a kid, a quiet kid who would give the shirt off his back to help someone. Now, I'd plot how to hurt someone who didn't pay what they owed and, if necessary, follow through with those plans. Sometimes I didn't know why I cried. Maybe deep inside it was guilt.

I figured I would have fewer problems if my girlfriend were more like my mother, a saved woman who prayed and didn't lie. So one night I told my girlfriend what she needed to do. Yeah, as scandalous as I was, I thought my life would get better if she got saved.

We drove to Mommy, my grandmother's house, so my girlfriend could get right with God. It was late, around 11:00 P.M. I remember my grandmother's house always smelling like old people—you know that mothball smell. Anyway, I sat in a chair in the living room as Mommy witnessed to my girlfriend in the dining room.

"Do you want to be saved?" my eighty-year-old grandmother whispered under the soft light.

"Yes," my girlfriend said. "I want to be saved."

But as Mommy began to lead my girlfriend in the Sinner's Prayer, I started tripping. I was crying and couldn't stop. "What you trippin' for?" I said to myself, afraid of what would come next. I got a flashback of being in church with my mother when I was a kid and watching people knocked around and falling out by the Holy Spirit. They'd start crying or yelling and slobbering all over themselves. I didn't want to get hit with that stuff.

Then my grandmother turned around and looked at me. She laid her hands on my shoulders: "Say yes."

"Yes," I said, relieved. All of a sudden I felt like a different person. I was saved. My little filly was saved. God just saved me!

I was juiced when we left Mommy's house. When we got home, I started calling everyone to tell them I was saved. My mother. My father. My brother. My clients. My friends. I couldn't believe it!

My girlfriend, a nurse's aide, and I bought a Bible and read it at home. At that time I was working in a small gym my father had opened. My girl and I scrounged together the little money we had, and I stopped hustling. We even tried not to have sex. But as time went on, we kept slipping up. So we got married in our attempt to live saved. We had a little chapel ceremony for my folks and hers. Six months later she got pregnant. By the time the baby came, I had started training for another bodybuilding competition and seeing private clients at my father's gym.

For a while, I managed to separate my new life from my old. When fillies called, I'd say, "I'm cool. I'm married now." When homeboys called, I'd say, "I ain't into that no more." They'd laugh and hang up.

I was still wearing gold around my neck and fingers. They probably figured I would crave the money I used to make or the excitement that life used to provide. Although I was really trying to live right, no one would reach out to teach me or disciple me so I would know how to live right. So no matter how many Bible verses I read, over the next five or six months I started slipping back into my old lifestyle. I took up a cleaner hustle, selling steroids that, unlike crack, didn't hurt anyone. But my frequent trips out of town caused problems with my wife. I started seeing old fillies and booking numbers again out of my father's gym where I worked. After months of being saved, I was deep into hustling again.

Money problems, not my illegal operation, forced my father to close his gym. Then I was fired from my job at a liquor store because, respecting ghetto code, I refused to snitch on an employee who was stealing money. Things at home were real bad, and I told my wife to go live with her father.

Around the same time (I was twenty-three), I opened up my own gym, a 900-square-foot room that rented for $400 a month. I had a little stash, money saved from the private bodybuilding lessons and my hustle. The gym was right smack in the middle of the hood, with a major crack house across the street. But it was cool because everybody there knew me, and, because they knew what I was capable of doing, nobody was gonna break into my gym and steal my stuff.

I named the gym The Iron Pit, the name of a weight room in a prison yard. I settled on that name because iron was the only thing that gave me relief. Pumping iron seemed to be the only time I could feel. I'd tell my gang, "I'm going to the gym to get my iron on." The hardness and the struggle of driving heavier and heavier weights was symbolic of the struggles in my life.

The only bright spot in my life at that time was my son. He would come to me when I walked through the door and throw his little arms around my legs. In him, I saw a new beginning—a chance for life without the hostility and anger that had become a part of me. My life was all screwed up. But with my son, I could go back to the beginning, my kind and gentle side.

That's why I was so upset when I learned my wife had gotten together with a drug dealer I didn't like, and his feelings were mutual. Over the next few weeks, I saw her around the neighborhood, wearing diamonds and fancy jewelry—"comin' up," as they say. She was with a dealer who had a personal vendetta against me for physically hurting him in a rough that we had years ago. She looked like she was reaping the benefits from being with him, but I knew his territory. I knew my son could be in danger, and I had to get him out of that environment.

I made the calls to round up a gang for a raid, complete with police officers and weapons. The day and time were arranged. The $800 deposit was paid on a job that would cost a couple of grand. I wanted my son out by any means necessary, and my wife safe. Whatever happened after that, happened.

On the day everything was supposed to go down, I got a phone call from my grandmother in Los Angeles at 3:00 P.M.

"You know I'm not one to pry in your business, but I was praying, and the Holy Spirit told me to call you," Granny said. I was listening to her and scrambling eggs.

"I don't know what you're doing, or getting ready to do, but the Lord didn't let me sleep last night," she said. "He told me one thing: Stand still and watch the salvation of the Lord. It's not going to turn out the way you think."

I hadn't spoken to Granny in a year, and now she called—the day everything was going down. What did she mean: "It's not going to turn out the way you think"? Was my son going to get hurt? I couldn't take that chance.

I slammed the receiver down and hurled the frying pan against the wall. I was upset—mad at my grandmother, mad at my wife, mad at the drug dealer for causing this mess, mad at God for getting in my way.

"Okay, I tried to do it Your way," I hollered. "We got saved. We went to church. We did what we was suppos'd to do. Didn't nobody teach me nothin'. Nobody came to see me."

I grabbed the phone and started dialing. A series of calls had to be made and money had to be paid.

"This can't go down tonight," I said. "Something's gonna happen. I don't know what. I heard through the grapevine that something's gonna happen to my boy, and I can't take that chance."

"What changed your mind? Are you alright?" said the voice on the other end.

"Just call it off and keep your deposit," I said. *Click.*

I stood in that kitchen, arguing with God like He was some cat on the street, for more than an hour. He said nothin', and soon I just got tired of yelling.

Then I heard faint words, something I'd heard in the gym sometimes, internally, not outside: *"Come home."*

I was torn up over my son and worn out by my life. "I'm tired of doing wrong," I told God. Even though I didn't say the Sinner's Prayer, I was ready to follow His advice and come home. It was then that I believe God welcomed me back that day. For the first time since I'd first gotten saved at my grandmother's home, I felt free.

I was twenty-five and made a deal with God: "You give me my son, and I'm gonna do the best I can to turn down wrong. When wrong comes to my door, I'm gonna turn it down."

I just came at Him straight like that, and I got serious about trusting God. No church. But I read the Word—religiously. When I tanned in my backyard before a bodybuilding competition, I'd pull out my Bible and wait for God to tell me which chapters to read. He "discipled" me one on one, and like any good teacher, He made sure I didn't miss important points.

To anyone watching, I must have looked like a crazy man in shorts, arguing with himself. But God and I weren't fighting; we were becoming friends.

"Read those verses," God would say.

"But I just did."

"Go back and read them again," He told me.

God was patient with me even when I made mistakes, like fooling around with women after my divorce.

That's how I learned about God's patience. It's as though God was saying, "Gary's like a baby. He just doesn't know any better."

My friendship with God grew, and after about six months, the Lord gave me a new word: Not only would I raise my son, but he would be greater than me. I didn't know how—but I thanked Him and held on to His word and also my promise.

People in my neighborhood would test me to see if I'd really changed. They'd send a filly in the gym or a hustler to try to tempt me. But I would turn their stuff down. Or they'd send illegal money into my gym and tell me I could make an interest-free loan on general principle. But I was faithful; I turned them down, too.

Getting back together with my son's mother was out, though I tried. She still wasn't ready to give up the streets. Still, I persuaded her that my son needed me to become a man. She let me visit him on a regular basis. Thursdays were our day. I'd pick him up, take him to the Pancake House, and help him with homework and reading. I would then pick him up every weekend to take him to church and stay the weekend at my house.

This was the arrangement for years. But all the while I prayed for more time with him. One night, his mother called and said my son could stay with me for a year.

Seven years passed. After divorcing my wife, I gained full custody of my son. By now, I had become an assistant pastor at a church my father opened. (He got saved the year before me.) Business at the gym was going well. People were built up by the weights and the Word in our weekly Bible studies open to anyone in the neighborhood.

One Communion Sunday at church, while I was holding the bread plate, God said: "The Iron Pit's coming to an end."

What? I thought to myself. *We've just started making a little cash. Maybe God wants me to preach full-time. But where's the money coming from? How am I going to survive?*

But I wasn't gonna argue with God. He'd been too faithful to me. So I began mapping out plans to sell the gym. That's when I heard Him say, "God's Gym." Again and again, I heard, "God's Gym."

In 1998, three years after I gained custody of my son, I changed the name of my gym from The Iron Pit to God's Gym. The welcome policy is still the same. When folks come inside, they know to leave their hustles and their mess outside. God's Gym is my world. It's a world where I want to help people climb out of the pit of depression, despair, and depravity. God has given me a lot more compassion and understanding, especially for people struggling with addictions and other things. When you've seen that kind of life, you understand that hurt people hurt people.

Some people have told me they wouldn't feel comfortable working out in my gym—the gospel music, the Bible study, God's way. And I say to them, "Well, do what you gotta do, go where you need to go, and learn what you need to learn. And if you change your mind, I'll still be here serving God. But The Iron Pit is closed. This is God's spot now."

God gave me a second chance after I walked away from Him. He returned my son. He stopped my anger. He taught me how to help, not hurt people. God wants us to know we can be completely satisfied if we look for our wealth, health, wisdom, and fulfillment in Him. Christ gives us peace that surpasses all understanding, and that's the very thing that I feel the whole world is looking for.[1]

Christ says, "I'll give you peace. I'll make you complete from within."[2] So you don't have to look for it in the games that people play to gain wealth and power in society.

Through God's Word and the world that I've built on His promises, I've found peace and a world where I belong. Everyone who desires to live within the boundaries of this world is welcome. Yes. It's a second chance at life and just one more sign of God's mercy, grace, and compassion that's new every day.

 **GARY SHIELDS** is founder and owner of God's Gym and resides in El Cerrito, California with his wife, daughter, and teenage son. He is the assistant pastor of Living Word Community Church and founder of Gospel Inner City Vision Evangelism (GIVE), a non-profit organization that seeks to reach out to under-privileged and undereducated inner-city youth and to foster racial, social and economic reconciliation in our society.

---

1. See John 14:27 in the Bible.
2. See Colossians 2:9 in the Bible.

RETURN OF MY LOST CHILDREN
Gail Hayes

Written by Linda Watkins

For most of my life, I didn't want children. I thought they would hinder my career. But I never expected a doctor to tell me I couldn't get pregnant. At age thirty-five, the news came. I had a closed womb, and my only option was surgery.

It was October 1990. My husband and I lived in Kaiserslautern in the Rhineland Pfalz area of Germany. He was a sergeant in the U.S. Army. I was the installation volunteer coordinator for our army community, which was 45 percent African-American. If a community event was needed, I rounded up volunteers and served as the official spokeswoman. In addition to my high-profile job, I coordinated fashion shows on the side.

What led me to the doctor in the first place was an irregular menstrual cycle. I was having only two periods a year compared to the twelve most women have. The pain during those cycles was so severe, I was bedridden the first day. In the past, I had visited several male gynecologists in America seeking help for my problem. Each one told me I had amenoria, a condition involving the absence of menses, which was normal for some women. But I decided to pursue another opinion in Germany. So I made an appointment with a female army doctor.

"I've never seen anything like this before," she gasped while examining me. "I tried to dilate your cervix but couldn't. There's a thick membrane covering it."

Before I could comment, the doctor left the room and didn't return for quite some time. When she did, I still couldn't squeeze a word in. She was on a roll.

"Gail, I've talked to some doctors, and we want to do surgery on you. We want to remove the membrane. It's why you're not having regular periods. It's also why you haven't gotten pregnant. The scar tissue over your cervix is quite amazing! It's like built-in birth control."

"Great," I interjected. I liked the idea of built-in birth control.

"Well, when do you want to do the surgery?"

Never, I thought. Why was she pressuring me anyway? Because she was thirty-five, pregnant, and excited? Well, I didn't want any babies.

"I want to discuss this with my husband," I stalled.

Deep down inside, however, I dreaded doing that because it meant confessing two abortions I had never told him about. They happened years before our marriage, not to mention long before I became a Christian.

At age twenty-one, my lifestyle was reckless. I was sexually active but did not use birth control. Totally focused on my job in Washington, D.C., I relished my work as central receptionist for a major Washington lobbyist firm. No one could have told me I would fall in love with the handsome young man who worked in the mailroom. He was eighteen years old and the color of dark-brown cinnamon. We were strictly friends until a pleasant date turned into a passionate love affair. So when I found out I was pregnant, I was livid!

The discovery came twelve weeks into the pregnancy when

my hourglass figure suddenly began to change. My stomach started feeling funny, and my well-defined waistline vanished. I was stunned because I'd worked so hard to keep a voluptuous shape. Although my boyfriend was happy—envisioning a long, fruitful life together—I, knowing better, was horrified. I was a social butterfly, and motherhood would lock me in a jar.

I knew babies could destroy a woman's life. I'd seen it with my own mother. She and my father had seven children of which I was the firstborn. Large families were the norm for many African-Americans who lived in the South in the 1950s. But to me, motherhood appeared to be thankless work. It seemed like the fate of a woman. I dreaded each time my mother got pregnant because it meant more work. As the oldest child and the oldest daughter, I became her primary assistant. She charged me with potty training each new baby. The newborns, who always wailed half the night, slept in my bedroom. Motherhood was horrible, and that was that! I vowed, when I got older, never to be captive to a life I hated.

So as I pondered the baby in my womb, only one thought came to mind: "This parasite isn't going to take my life away or make me dependent on a man."

This was my body and, frankly, my boyfriend had no say. Like a missile aimed at an enemy target, I aborted that child. The procedure was surprisingly efficient, and I quickly returned to my normal activities. Remorse? There was none. I didn't know a fetus was a life (until I became a Christian seven years later).

I was equally nonchalant about my second abortion the following year. But life was more complex then because I was in transition. Determined to finish my college degree as cheaply as possible, I had opted to attend a state university in Fayetteville, North Carolina, which was near my parents' home. Living with strict parents was hard enough. If they knew I was pregnant, it'd be harder. So I didn't tell anyone about the pregnancy. I didn't even tell my boyfriend, the same young man who had gotten me pregnant the first time. Instead, I secretly went to an abortion clinic in town.

This time the experience was different. I felt emotionally empty and alone. Maybe because no one came with me, unlike the first abortion. Or because I was the only African-American in the place; all the doctors, nurses, and other patients were white. Or maybe it was because the procedure wasn't as smooth. At one point, something went wrong. I felt the doctor digging inside of me and struggling to pull something out. I sat up to see what it was. Immediately, a frantic nurse slammed me back on the table.

My body ached after that procedure, but I tried to act like everything was normal. I eased off that abortion table, caught a bus, and went to math class. But for weeks I felt drained and depressed. I shut out everyone close, from my boyfriend who wanted to marry me to friends and family members. Then I secretly tried to commit suicide. Amazingly, I never linked my depression to the abortions. Eventually, I pulled myself up through schoolwork and a series of jobs.

Fourteen years later, telling my husband about those abortions was one of the hardest things I ever had to do. I feared he'd reject me as his wife if he knew what I had done. No doubt, the second abortion caused the thick membrane over my cervix. The night of my visit to the American army doctor, I gingerly broached the subject.

"Well, they want to do surgery on me, honey," I began. His eyes filled with concern. "She thinks it might be because of what happened earlier."

"What's that?" he asked.

I could hardly breathe when I told him. When he started sobbing, I felt so bad.

"All the time you were going through this and hid it from me. You never said anything about it," he said, crying.

But instead of condemnation, my strong, handsome husband held me in his arms. "How horrible that must have been for you. Baby, God has forgiven you. You've got to forgive yourself."

Forgive myself? I thought as I started to cry with him. I had no feelings of attachment toward those children. I'd never considered them as mine. They were with the Lord, and He could take better care of them than I ever could. Nevertheless, I carefully chose my reply.

"I don't know if I can forgive myself. I feel so detached," I confessed. "That's why I don't want children. I'm afraid I'll be a terrible mother."

But I knew my husband wanted children, so I proposed, "Maybe we can adopt. That's safe."

"I'm not ready for that, honey. But I will tell you this: If God closed your womb, He'll open it. You won't have anyone cutting on you. When those doctors call, tell them no!"

Boy, was I relieved! My husband was so understanding. As a result, I didn't have the surgery. We simply went on with our lives.

The next year our income soared with my husband's new job. He began working with an American military contractor that provided battle simulation training for the U.S. Army. I continued in my position as volunteer coordinator, and we moved outside of the army community into a lovely old farmhouse near a tranquil lake. We were the only African-Americans in that small German town.

It was there that I started to contemplate my life, maybe because age forty was several years away. I realized I had accepted Jesus Christ as Lord six years before but had never really committed to learn about Him. When I pledged to do so that year, I was serious. The first thing God told me to do was quit my job, and I did. He said my work had become the center of my world and that He wanted the driver's seat.

Life slowed down considerably after leaving my job. I opened a small boutique and began to sell my own hand-painted silk scarves. I also got involved in a Christian women's group, attended Bible study classes, and frequented Christian conferences. That lifestyle sufficed for a few years, but eventually I became depressed. Was it because I was no longer Gail Hayes, star of the community? Or hand-painting scarves wasn't really getting it for me?

Whatever the answer, I knew that I needed to talk to someone about it. One day when I was near rock bottom, that someone was a Christian friend. An African-American "sister" married to a U.S. soldier, she had tremendous faith in God.

"I don't know what it is. I'm hurting, I'm grieving. Nothing I do makes me happy," I confided one day when I visited her home.

Immediately, she offered to pray for me as I sat in a chair. That dear, sweet woman prayed over me for an hour. But after she stopped praying, a sharp picture entered my mind.

I was lying in a hospital bed in a strange place, adorned in a white gown as bright as the sun. Beside the bed was a huge archway. Inside the archway, as far as the eye could see, were tiny coffins side by side. Then I heard the voice of God.

"Behold, all the babies that have been aborted."

Gazing upward, I saw an endless row of coffins leading up to heaven.

"Behold," God said again, as a large gold finger opened the first two boxes.

There before my eyes were two live babies, a boy and a girl. The finger lifted up each child and gently placed them in my arms.

God revealed, "You have been grieving for your lost children." I was surprised and relieved.

"Since you have heard My voice and been obedient in recent years, I shall restore them to you," God said.

"How Lord? I have a closed womb, and I'm almost thirty-eight years old."

"I am God."

With that, the vision ended. Still on my knees and totally astonished, I searched for my friend who was standing right by me.

"God said He's gonna give me children!" I told her.

"Okay, Gail." She didn't blink an eye.

"But I'm too old to have children. I'm almost thirty-eight years old."

She quickly reminded me of Sarah in the Bible who God

enabled to give birth at an old age. But this was now, I thought driving home. Nevertheless, when I arrived I fetched a journal and recorded my experience: *April 17, 1993—Vision with Two Babies.*

In addition to receiving that incredible vision, something else happened at my friend's house. It didn't take long to notice my depression was gone! It was like a great cloud of gloom had been lifted off me. Gradually, my life changed and ushered in a new sense of purpose. God gave me the concept for a new book about women and their self-image. Later it would be called *Daughters of the King.*

In addition to writing, I began speaking at Christian meetings. Then came new consulting work for the U.S. government. As needed, I coordinated special programs like Black History Month and Women's History Month events, and trained adults through the Office of Personnel Management. I couldn't believe that, once again, I was high-profile Gail. This went on for two whole years.

It would have been longer if my husband hadn't been laid off from his job after the company he worked for lost its army contract. With no steady income, we had no choice but to return to America. My husband and I ended up in Durham where we had family.

By God's grace, he was able to find a job but had to take a 75 percent pay cut. Still, he insisted that I not work in order to finish writing my book. Our new two-bedroom apartment in an integrated section of Durham was a far cry from our spacious farmhouse in Germany. But we were determined to survive and trusted God to help us.

And survive we did. I even finished my book and decided to publish it myself. On October 18, 1995, the day after my fortieth birthday, the printer called to request the final payment for the book copies. My husband was so supportive, he rearranged his work schedule to go with me to the bank. That morning, we left our apartment with great expectation.

"I'd like to withdraw $1,163," I told the teller.

"I'm sorry, ma'am, but you only have $45 in your account."

I couldn't believe it! But there it was in black and white on the teller's screen—$45.

"What are we gonna do?" I turned to my husband. By this time I was bawling, not to mention holding up the line behind us.

"Honey, we've got to go," he warmly replied.

"What about the book?" I said, crying.

"What's the title of the book, honey?"

"Daughters of the King."

"Then the King will bring the money. Let's go!"

Never had I seen my husband's faith so strong and mine so weak. I thought I was the warrior when it came to having faith. But that morning, my husband ministered to me in front of all those people. It hit me like a ton of bricks all the way home. And so did his incredible love for me.

My man walked me into our apartment, made sure I was settled, then headed out the door to work. It was sunny as I watched him walk across the parking lot. I was standing at our balcony, which overlooked the parking lot of our complex. That's when I really saw my husband, as if for the first time in months.

He looked so defeated and sad as his six-foot frame hobbled toward our car. My husband's broad shoulders were slumped. His strong-featured face exuded pain. I could tell his hip was hurting that morning. We both knew he needed a hip replacement. But there was something more. My husband hated his job at the computer company he worked for.

Look at this man who'd go to a place he hated to take care of me, I thought.

Compassion filled my heart as well as an overwhelming sense of love for him. I dropped to my knees and wept uncontrollably, realizing I had been so selfish. Throughout our marriage, I had put my needs before my husband's. Time after time, I neglected his desires and sometimes even him. Although he hadn't said it in years, I knew his greatest wish was to be a father. At that moment, guilt pierced my heart and I desired to submit to my husband's will. Kneeling before our black velvet love seat, I cried out to God.

"Father, it seems a shame to rob this dear, precious man of the gift of fatherhood. I ask that You forgive me, Father. Your maid-servant humbles herself and asks, if it be Your perfect will, please open my womb . . . And about the book, if You have to rain money down from heaven, I expect that."

From that moment on, I decided to put my husband second after God. A new surge of faith filled my soul, and I was expect-ing miracles. Within a week, the first one came. A member of my church who was visiting our home for Bible study said God wanted her to ask me how my book was progressing. When I told her my financial problem, she inquired about how much I needed. The next day, she left a $1,500 check on my doorstep. Two months later was an even bigger prize—I was pregnant!

My husband knew before I did. He said my body tempera-ture was warmer than usual. We also had been much more pas-sionate with each other. After my prayer, the Lord increased my desire for my husband. Every aspect of our marriage intensified, even lovemaking. But while he was elated about the pregnancy, I had mixed emotions.

"God! What are You doing to me? I'm forty years old. You said You would give me the book and then I'd minister to women."

"Didn't you say My perfect will?" God replied.

"Yes. But what am I gonna do with a baby?"

"You're going to be a wonderful mother."

Joshua Matthew entered the earth on September 8, 1996. The first name of our precious little boy means "Jehovah saves." His middle name, Matthew, means "gift from God." Amazingly, moth-erhood was as natural for me as breathing. For the first time in my life, I felt fulfilled, completely satisfied. I discovered I could be a mother, a writer, and a minister.

My husband and I settled into our new lifestyle like old pros. I even returned to consulting work, until I found out I was pregnant again! Most women would have been ecstatic, but I am not most women.

"God, what am I gonna do with two babies?" I fumed. "How will I handle two children? I'm forty-two years old!"

Money was extremely tight, and my family was already crammed in our two-bedroom apartment. Four people would be too much. All I could think to do was write out my frustrations. So I sat at my desk with a pen and paper. But I was too upset to write. So I opened the top drawer and started cleaning.

I wasn't really looking for anything. The old journal found me. It was my trusty diary from Germany, which I hadn't seen in years. I had long forgotten its contents. That's why my heart nearly stopped when I came to a most peculiar entry: *April 17, 1993— Vision with Two Babies*. Buried in my memory, the meaning of the words quickly surfaced. God said I would have two children, a boy and a girl.

Nine months later, our daughter Gabrielle Christina was born. We named her Gabrielle because it means "the Lord is my strength." Christina means "anointed."

I learned so much about God through the birth of my children. I always knew He was righteous and merciful. But I never realized how faithful He was. Now I know when God makes a promise, He keeps it. And no unbelief, fear, or amnesia on our part can halt the mighty works of the Lord. God's so awesome; He speaks to the barren, and they conceive.

The Lord allowed me to conceive without surgery and returned my long-lost children to me. He forgave me for my abortions, and I eventually forgave myself. At the time I ended those pregnancies, I strongly believed that a fetus was nothing more than excess tissue. Now I know that abortion is wrong, it's the taking of a human life. Pregnant women should seek other options that are best for them and their children.

Over the years, God taught me that no career or material possession can take the place of my babies. Even when my silk robes are soiled with peanut butter and milk, I still thank God for a second chance at motherhood.

 **GAIL HAYES** is the founder and executive director of Daughters of the King Ministries, Inc. She is a conference speaker who ministers in a down-to-earth manner. Her mandate from God is to bring together women of many nations to pray, worship, and lift up the name of Jesus. Hayes is the author of three books: *Daughters of the King, Honoring Your First Gift,* and *The Intercessor's Numerical Prayer Guide.* She lives in Durham, North Carolina with her husband and two children.

6

THE GOD WHO STICKS CLOSER THAN A BROTHER

Black fraternity members say, "I got your back." No matter how big the task, how rough the blows, or how great the sacrifice, every man on the pledge line helps his brother cross over. They bear one another's burdens—seen and unseen—to ensure that none are left behind.

Taking the backs of our brothers and sisters is a lesson for all African-Americans. It's exactly what Jesus does for us twenty-four/ seven. Like a shadow on a sunny day, our Lord sticks closer than a brother. He listens to our problems, lightens our load, and sends us lifelines when we don't even know it.

When Jesus died on the cross, He said, "I got your back." Through Him we have a chance to cross over into heaven. The stories in this chapter illustrate that Jesus is with us and wants the human race to receive God's blessings for our lives.

Be strong and of good courage; do not be
afraid, nor be dismayed, for the Lord your
God is with you wherever you go.

JOSHUA 1:9b (NKJV)

MORE THAN A MAN
Dr. Jawanza Kunjufu

Written by Linda Watkins

When I was a boy and then a young man, I looked to Black men for love. Not just any kind of love, unconditional love. Like many African-American male children growing up in the inner city, I yearned for Black male role models and their unwavering support.

My father—the first man in my life—was also my first role model. He was six feet tall, 185 pounds, and worked two jobs. He painted houses from 7:00 A.M. until 2:00 P.M., then ran home, showered, and dressed for his post office job afternoons and evenings. My father and mother, also a postal employee, worked hard to raise my sister and me in a comfortable home. Our family lived in a nice neighborhood in Chicago where everybody on the block knew one another.

The year I turned twelve, my parents divorced. I stayed with my mother but didn't feel like I lost a father because we saw each other almost every weekend. My father supported me financially and came to all of my track meets. That was impressive because many times he was the only father there, and I had thirty teammates.

On the flip side, my father had high expectations that were tough to live up to. I remember when I was in a championship track meet in high school. I finished second, but that was alright because I was struggling to breathe by the end of the race. All I wanted at that point was to see my father's proud face.

"You could have won that race," he responded unemotionally.

I was hurt, angry, and thought to myself, *I could barely breathe, and you're on my case!*

My father was equally demanding when it came to my grades. Throughout my elementary and high school years, I compared myself academically to my sister. She used to get Bs and Cs and that was acceptable to my father. So I thought it was acceptable for me. But he constantly rode my back when I got anything less than an A.

"Well, I just know you're an A student," he insisted.

Needless to say, I thought my father was picky, unfair, and unrealistic when I was growing up. His love for me seemed conditional, based on how well I did, not that I was his only son. During my late teenage years, the tension between us grew as I began to form my own views about the world and my future.

When I entered Illinois State University as a freshman in 1970, it was the height of the Black Power Movement in America. I was seventeen years old, politically conscious, and eager to get involved in the struggle to advance Black people. The campus environment exposed me to a rich array of dynamic Black leaders like Stokely Carmichael, Haki Madhubuti, Amiri Baraka, and Maulana Karenga. Before long, I was going to rallies, reading books on Black history and culture, and joining groups that were active in the movement. Black people became my passion, helping our community my career goal. And I was militant about that.

Of course, this was not in line with my father's plans for my life. He wanted me to go to college and graduate with a business degree. He wanted me to work for a white corporation. He wanted me to live in the suburbs and have the kind of life he had wanted for himself. But I didn't want that. My plan was to work for a Black organization, not a white corporation, after college and move away from everything that was contrary to the Black struggle.

That's why I changed my name from Jerome Brown to Jawanza Kunjufu my junior year in college. I worked with an African-centered organization and several members gave me my new name because Jawanza means "dependable" and Kunjufu "cheerful." It replaced the European name that my parents had given me at birth.

I also left the traditional Black church after joining the movement. I had attended Black churches throughout my childhood years and said the Sinner's Prayer when I was seven. Each summer, I received a heavy dose of church because my parents shipped my sister and me to Nacogdoches, Texas, by Amtrak train to spend vacations with our Holy Ghost–filled grandmother.

But in the movement, politically conscious brothers and sisters believed that Christianity was "the white man's religion." They taught that Christianity and the church were responsible, in part, for the mess Black people were in. Now they weren't anti-God. Many considered themselves to be spiritual. But we all knew those images of a white, blond-haired, blue-eyed Jesus Christ were a lie. That image was ingrained in our minds because it was all over our churches on crosses, hand fans, and Sunday school books when we were growing up. It seemed like Black church folks were caught up in spending eternal life with a white Jesus in heaven. Meanwhile, white people who run the world were living the good life here on earth.

So Christianity did not have an acceptable place in the Black Power Movement. We often joked about how weak Christians seemed, and we openly criticized Black ministers who took advantage of poor people's money and lonely women, including other people's wives.

The Black Power Movement gave me new thoughts and new role models. After graduating from college in 1974, I worked full-time for a powerful Black leader who headed up a well-known organization in Chicago. It had an Africentric school, bookstore, publishing company, food cooperative, and cultural programs. The leader was eleven years older than me, and I really looked up to him. Not only did I look up to him, I began to pattern my life after his. He was a well-known speaker, so I desired to speak publicly. He was a writer, so I began to write about African-American issues. I was so dedicated to this man that I agreed to the group's communal living arrangement and worked for a salary of $250 a month, since most of my basic needs were met. That really tripped my father when he found out.

"You have a college degree, and this is what you're making? That's crazy," he said, reminding me that I made $250 a month as a paperboy and stock clerk when I was fourteen.

But I was happy. In fact, I was no longer "I." I was "we." And we—all the members of the group—were working to empower our community. I served in various roles, depending on the need. Among them were accountant, principal of our school, and manager of the publishing company. After several years, I became a spokesman for the organization. I spoke locally and nationally, flying to rallies and conferences in cities like Milwaukee, St. Louis, and Detroit. Everything seemed to be going well. Then in 1980 a crisis hit. A thorn of jealousy rose up within our group. I was the one who got stabbed.

Suddenly, "brothers" who I had worked with for years began to distrust me. Insecure about my growing popularity, my mentor started censoring where I went and what I said. Naturally, I felt betrayed and insulted. Over the years, I had given him my money. I'd given him my time and talent. I'd even given him my heart. I loved that man like a father. I couldn't help thinking that just as my real father had failed to loved me unconditionally, the second great man in my life also betrayed me. The hurt and disappointment were too much to bear, so I left the organization. At age twenty-seven, I applied to graduate schools and ventured out on my own.

A few weeks later, the group called me. That was a surprise. Apparently, a children's organization in New Orleans had called them looking for me. They wanted me to speak at their national conference. The group I had left tried to offer them another speaker but the children's organization refused to accept anyone else. At first that stunned me because my former role model always told me that my notoriety was because of my affiliation with his group, not because of me. But here was this children's organization that wanted me to speak, whether or not I was with the group. I jumped at the opportunity and flew to New Orleans several weeks later.

The day of my arrival was a sunny, Deep South hot August day. The conference was held at a university, thankfully with air-conditioned buildings. Four hundred people had gathered in the auditorium for my session entitled "Developing Positive Self-Images and Discipline in Black Children." After the first half of my presentation, the audience gave me a standing ovation.

This was a major breakthrough for me because for years I also thought my success as a speaker was predicated on my relationship to my former mentor's group. Immediately, a fountain of thankfulness bubbled inside of me, and I felt compelled to go outside and simply thank God! God, you might say? Yes, God. The same God I hadn't paid attention to in years. For some reason, deep inside my soul I knew what had happened in that auditorium was nothing *but* the Lord. Maybe it was all that "churching" I had as a child. Intuitively, I knew that God was the source of my help.

So during my fifteen-minute break, I walked out of the building and was greeted by a sunny, clear, blue sky. I found an empty parking lot nearby and raised my arms high in the air. There was no one there but me and the Lord.

"Thank You, God!" I shouted, looking up at the sky. I felt like the writer of Psalm 121 who said, *I will lift up my eyes to the hills. Where does my help come from? My help comes from the Lord.*

Suddenly, I felt a wave of peace, joy, and power wash over me. As I looked up, I felt God looking down at me.

"You never belonged to your father. You never belonged to your mentor. You were always Mine," the Lord said.

"I'm your Father, and the One who loves you unconditionally. You are My child. I will never leave nor forsake you. You made a mistake and gave your life to somebody else. Don't ever do that again. Don't ever let anyone control your life again. I will give you everything you ask for. I will open up doors for you. I'll open up more and more doors."

Tears began to stream down my face, and I felt so grateful to God. I was filled with peace and a greater sense of confidence. The Lord had taken the time to look down on *me*. Within seconds, He had taught and scolded me. He gently reminded me that my real mistake had been looking for love in all the wrong places. It was like God reciting the passage in Jeremiah 29:11 where it basically says, I alone know the plans that I have for you, plans of prosperity and not disaster. Plans for the future that you've hoped for.

I looked up at the sky and promised God that I would never worship another man again. I told Him I would never allow my emotions or self-esteem to be controlled by someone else. I knew He had a plan for my life, and I needed to look to Him for guidance.

That day changed my life. When I returned to Chicago I immediately looked for a church home because I wanted to be with the Lord and learn more about Him. I began to walk and talk with God daily by reading the Bible and praying. Over the past twenty years, I've developed a personal relationship with the Lord, and He has blessed and prospered me as He promised.

God has opened doors to speaking engagements all over the world. He has helped me build my Black communications company into a multimillion-dollar business. He has given me a beautiful wife, two sons, and a vibrant church home. I know that everything good that has happened to me is because I'm connected to God.

While I still struggle to connect with my earthly father, I've come to understand and appreciate him more. Because I now have sons, I know why he rode my back so hard. My father knew what it was going to take in order to make me successful. That's why he wouldn't accept anything less.

But I've learned over the years to stop looking to him or any other man for unconditional love. God is our source of unwavering love. He's closer than a father, brother, or any role model. God is more than a man. He's even larger than heroes of Black history.

While I still love my culture greatly, and my life's work is raising Black consciousness, I've married my culture to my relationship with Jesus Christ (who, by the way, is not some weak, blond-haired, blue-eyed wimp on a cross. He's not white or Black. He's Spirit). As much as I love Malcolm X, Queen Nzingha, and Harriet Tubman, Africentricity can't fill the void during major challenges like when your marriage is in trouble, your children are wayward, and you have more bills than revenue. At times like these, you're going to need something stronger, something higher. You're going to need the Lord.

 **DR. JAWANZA KUNJUFU** is president of African American Images, a communications company in Chicago. He is a nationally recognized educational consultant, a speaker, and the author of numerous books. Dr. Kunjufu's life goal is to empower African-Americans on four levels: bringing them to Christ, freeing them from racism, freeing them economically, and freeing them from disease. He and his wife are members of Living Word Christian Center in Chicago.

CONQUERING FEAR

Sharon Flake

Written by Linda Watkins

Sitting onstage with actress Della Reese, author Virginia Hamilton, and other well-known writers, I gazed at the sea of multicultural faces. All of us had gathered for the Coretta Scott King Awards Breakfast at the American Library Association's annual conference in New Orleans.

"We are proud to present the 1999 Coretta Scott King/John Steptoe New Talent Award to Sharon Flake for her young adult book, *The Skin I'm In*," the speaker announced.

Amid thunderous applause, I rose from my seat to walk to the podium as nine hundred people watched. As soon as the elegant black-and-gold award touched my hand, I was overcome with emotion and began to cry. I thanked the literary world during my three-minute acceptance speech and told everyone that God had blessed my life. Just one year earlier, my fear of public speaking might have stopped me from claiming that award onstage. But since that time, God had delivered me from much of my fear and anxiety. On that monumental day, I was not afraid. I was grateful.

My battle with fear began when I was a little girl. Growing up in North Philadelphia, I was the fifth child and third girl of six brothers and sisters. Although my parents were not professional people—my father installed pipes for a gas company, my mother worked in people's homes—our household was filled with rich conversation, laughter, and opinions.

My parents religiously read newspapers, watched television, and listened to radio. Current events and convictions were as common as good food around our dinner table. Early on, my brothers, sisters, and I learned that outside our front door was a critical world, a world that would judge us based on what we knew and how we behaved.

Young and impressionable, I internalized a lot of what I heard around the house and began to judge myself by a large stick, one that would later prove too hard for me to live up to.

I became insecure, developed low self-esteem, and constantly worried about what others thought of me. Outwardly I seemed bold, even funny, but inside I was anxious and afraid. As I grew, fear began to rob me of precious opportunities.

Like the time I turned down two invitations to my high school prom. One prospective date was really cute, but I decided not to go. "You're not a good dancer, Sharon. Everyone will laugh at you," a voice whispered inside my head.

Later, I regretted not going when I saw the beautiful prom pictures in my yearbook. I could see from all the smiling faces the wonderful time that I missed.

During my junior year in college, fear caused me to blow a lucrative newspaper internship. The internship was scheduled for the fall semester, but in September I never showed up. I had convinced myself the day before, "You just talked your way into the job. You're really not a good writer."

The same thought lingered after graduating from college. That's why I never even considered writing as a career following graduation.

While college professors had encouraged me to write professionally, I opted to work as a house mother at a temporary housing facility for youth. The teenagers were transitioning from the court system into family homes and group homes. I would wake them up, make sure they got to school, oversee evening meals, and ensure they went to bed. After leaving that position, I took on another one working with youth in foster care. I stayed there for eight years. However, I could not shake the feeling that God wanted me to be a writer. So at home at night I would pore over grammar books, believing that perfecting that skill would give me the confidence to do what I felt God called me to do. I joined a writing group and wrote short articles for small publications. But all the while, I felt that I didn't have what it took.

By the time I turned thirty, my fears snowballed into anxiety. Being diagnosed with mytro valve prolapse triggered it. That's a condition when the valve to your heart sticks. I began to take medicine but believed I was really going to die. So all of my fears converged into one, the fear of death.

Without warning, I began to have panic attacks. I'm not talking about the normal stress people experience every day. Panic attacks, a symptom of anxiety, hit you suddenly. One second you feel great; the next you think you're losing your mind. Tightness in the throat, heart palpitations, extreme terror, and mental anguish—these are just several ingredients of a panic attack. The worse thing is you feel powerless to control what's happening to you. Everyday things you used to do with ease suddenly become major tasks.

That's what happened to me one day in 1985. I jumped out of bed, got dressed, and headed out the door to my job at a foster care agency.

"I feel really good. It's gonna be a great day," I said around 8:30 A.M., locking the door of my third-floor apartment.

But inner sunshine turned to gloom by the time I reached step four of the staircase. Suddenly, my heart started beating fast and negative thoughts flooded my mind: "Sharon, you're not gonna make it. You're gonna have a panic attack just like yesterday."

Gripping the wooden rail with both hands, I tried to convince myself that I'd be okay. But I felt like a prisoner on death row walking down a long hall to his execution. With each step, the inmate knows something hideous awaits him, but he still tries to comfort himself by thinking everything's going to be all right.

In just two minutes, I'd gone from confident to petrified and felt as if I was on the verge of having a nervous breakdown. Getting to work was no longer my main focus; rather, making it down six stairs. Not to reach my compact car parked on the street, but to get to the door of my girlfriend's apartment. She lived on the second floor. If anyone could help me, I hoped she could.

Step by step the tension within me grew as my trickling tears turned into suffocating sobs.

"What's wrong with me? Why can't I control myself?" I cried, finally reaching the platform of the second floor.

I used my last ounce of courage left to bang on my girlfriend's door. Thank God she was at home! Someone else probably would have called the police if they saw a bawling Black woman hanging around their door. But my spiritual dreadlocked friend hugged me tightly and led me inside. She fed my grieving soul soothing herbal tea and Bible Scriptures.

Surprisingly, the Bible Scriptures calmed me down. Twenty minutes later, I left for work and made it through the day without having another panic attack. But I was still scared because I knew one could strike at any time. However, I have never been the type of person to sit around and wait for things to happen to me, so I decided to take things into my own hands: I sought professional help.

Recognizing that traditional medicine doesn't have all of the answers, I began my search for wellness with a holistic doctor. She was a calm, petite sister with a short Afro. She insisted that the solution to my problem was "manipulating the negative energy" in my body.

When I visited her office, she laid me down in towels and massaged from my shoulders down to my feet. Then she placed small stones across my back. The warm, smooth stones seemed to have some effect because I felt more relaxed afterward. However, by the time I got home, I was anxious again for no apparent reason.

Next I went to a hypnotist, a calm, peaceful white gentleman in his sixties.

"Regressive therapy is the key to your solution," he reassured.

Although he hypnotized me twice, taking me back to my childhood, he still couldn't tell me why I was having panic attacks. I stopped going after the second session because we met in the man's home. As a single woman, I didn't feel comfortable being semiconscious in a stranger's house.

So I turned to my medical doctor for help. He immediately prescribed sedatives for my anxiety. He suggested that I take them "as long as needed." But I certainly wasn't about to get hooked on drugs, so I stopped taking them after two capsules.

I easily spent several hundred dollars searching for a cure for my anxiety. Yet when the anxiety continued, and a cure seemed nowhere in sight, I finally decided to rely on the Lord. When I was a child, old folks at church used to say, "When in trouble, turn to the Lord." I hadn't attended a church regularly in years, but something inside of me compelled me to read the Bible at the same time I visited those doctors, hypnotists, and others.

But I didn't fully believe God could heal me. With little to lose, I decided to find out if God could do for me what the Bible said He could. My first step was to find a church that could help me reconnect with the Lord. Luckily I found one not too far from where I lived.

It was a Black Baptist church with a good reputation and a good gospel choir. At its Sunday worship service I discovered that soulful songs and Bible Scriptures calmed my nerves. They gave me inner strength Sunday after Sunday as I attended church regularly for the first time in years. I began to look to God for guidance and to trust Him like never before.

Pretty soon I carried a Bible with me all the time. At work I'd flip through its pages for encouragement. It was as if God would lead me to specific Scriptures each time I opened the Book. Several times He took me to the forty-third chapter of the book Isaiah.

There it says: *"Do not remember the former things, nor consider the things of old. Behold, I will do a new thing, now it shall spring; shall you not know it? I will even make a road in the wilderness and rivers in the desert . . . because I give waters in the wilderness and rivers in the desert, to give drink to My people, My chosen. This people I have formed for Myself; they shall declare My praise"* (vv. 18–21 NKJV).

Hope filled my heart every time I read that passage. It was like hearing God say, "Sharon, things are going to change in your life. Until then, I'll sustain you. You can trust Me."

In response, I looked to God each morning. "Lord, get me through this day. Help me trust You. Don't let me go crazy," I prayed.

And day by day, God pulled me through until six months later my panic attacks were gone.

Miraculously I regained my confidence and began to work at a state university in Pittsburgh. As a public relations specialist for my alma mater, I finally had a chance to write professionally. I wrote a lot of press releases and helped professors get media coverage for their research. Working behind the scenes in a job I enjoyed, it seemed like my anxiety had left for good. For years I didn't have another panic attack and lived a relatively peaceful life.

Eventually, I decided to pursue a more challenging job. A prestigious position was vacant—director of public relations at the university's business school. At first I was nervous about seeking the job, but after praying, I believed that God wanted me to have it. I'd been in public relations for seven years and was ready to try something new. So I applied for the job and got it!

I was so excited until the magnitude of my new responsibilities hit me during my second week of work. That's when it dawned on me there was no supervisor to hide behind. I was highly visible and totally accountable. The fear that gripped my stomach that day took me back to my high school years when I refused to go to the prom because I didn't want people to see how I danced. Now I was out front and in the spotlight.

Oh, my God, what have I done? Everybody's looking at me, I thought each time I walked down the halls of the business school.

Most of my colleagues didn't have a clue about my battle with fear and anxiety. To them I appeared friendly, polished, and outgoing. They had no idea that I would shut my office door sometimes and cry and pray for help. They couldn't imagine how small and incompetent I felt despite years of experience in the public relations field. The voice of condemnation had returned, "Sharon, you're not good enough."

Intentionally I avoided public speaking opportunities. I'd think of ways to get out of being in the spotlight. On occasions when I had to speak to a group, I'd beg God to get me through. My way of coping was to simply avoid thinking about the event until absolutely necessary. Often, that meant the day before or the morning of the activity. By then I'd be even more scared because I knew I wasn't prepared for the task at hand. The same thing happened when I had to run meetings.

One time I was asked to head a committee charged with developing a marketing plan for the school. There we were sitting around a table, me and several other professionals from the university. We all had the same rank and title, but my other colleagues were much more confident than I was. Before walking into the meeting I had already convinced myself that leading the group would be like trying to reign wild horses. I asked God to give me strength, but I still lost control of that meeting. As my colleagues jockeyed for center stage, nothing was accomplished until one of them finally stepped in and took over my role as facilitator.

During and after the meeting I was totally humiliated. Once again I began to ask God why I was there and why He wouldn't speak to my heart and tell me to leave that place.

"If *You* brought me to this job, where are You, God? Why are *You* letting this happen to me?" I cried. A coworker I was close to stopped by just in time to let me cry on her shoulder and to remind me that I was good at my job and had what it took to do the tasks at hand.

That wasn't the first time I had wanted to quit, nor would it be the last. Off and on for four years I cried in that position but still managed to hold on to it. Every time I planned to jump ship, someone encouraged me to stay. At the roughest points, I'd receive a glowing evaluation or hear an uplifting message on Christian radio.

One day a charismatic evangelist preached, "If God puts you somewhere, don't leave until He tells you to go!"

Not until later would I realize God was with me all along, using coworkers, ministers, and job evaluations to push me past my fears. In the midst of sorrow, the Lord gave me small but meaningful victories.

One year I entered the August Wilson Short Story Contest in Pittsburgh and won first prize. I had written a story about twin girls—one dark, the other light skinned—and how the world treated them differently based on their skin color. The same year I won a competition sponsored by the national children's magazine, *Highlights*. One of the benefits of winning was a chance to submit a story to a famous children's author for review. I chose a short piece I had written on a girl working through issues with her mother and father.

Little did I know that story would sharpen my writing skills and give me the courage to write another novel about a young girl called *The Skin I'm In*. The book is about a dark-skinned girl's journey to self-acceptance. Its main character, Maleeka Madison, is a seventh grader at an inner-city school who discovers her beauty and talent with the help of her strong Black teacher, Miss Saunders.

I wrote the book to affirm my own daughter who has a beautiful chocolate-brown complexion, which, unfortunately, is seldom celebrated by our society and even the Black community. But after *The Skin I'm In* was published, I realized the book's main characters reflected my dual personality. Like Maleeka, I had often felt small and unempowered in a hostile world. But the Miss Saunders in me was trying to help my wounded inner child discover her strengths.

By God's grace, the first publisher who read *The Skin I'm In* wanted to publish it. That was 1998, the year my life finally found balance. My anxiety had ceased. I was much more comfortable at work and totally committed to God whom I leaned on every day.

I remember singing in church one Sunday, *Lord, if You can use anything, You can use me.* For years I had sung that song, but this time I really meant it. A new belief had welled up inside: God had a purpose for my life and could use me even with my flaws.

The first sign came a year later when *The Skin I'm In* became an overnight success. The American Library Association named it a Best Book for Young Adult Readers in 1999. The New York City Public Library listed the novel among its Top Ten Books for Youth. *Publishers Weekly* even named me one of seven new authors to watch. Immediately I was thrust into the spotlight. Book signing offers, speaking engagements, and mail flooded my world. Local radio and television stations called and so did Black Entertainment Television (BET) in Washington, D.C.

Months before I would have panicked over all the attention, but a new surge of confidence filled my soul instead. Peace replaced fear, excitement overtook anxiety. For the first time in my life, I was actually relaxed in front of a television camera. That was the moment I realized that God had healed me. Me, the woman who used to run from speaking engagements. Me, the one who used to cry at the thought of being in the spotlight. Me, who years before lacked the confidence to walk down a flight of stairs.

From time to time, I may still get a little anxious when I have to face the public. But it's different now because I know that God will carry me through whatever I have to do. God is bigger than my fears. Today when I'm not working in public relations, I cherish the opportunity to talk about *The Skin I'm In*. Each time I have a platform to promote the book, I also find myself telling audiences about God.

I let them know, young and old, that God helped me conquer many of my fears. It didn't happen overnight. It happened over years; years when hypnotists and medical and holistic doctors couldn't help me. The only one who could was the Lord.

During that awful season in my life, I learned that God is real. Even when we hit rock bottom and think He's nowhere in sight, the Lord is pulling us through day by day. The more we seek and trust Him, the more He controls our lives and steers us toward the unique purpose He created us for. God created me to be a writer, and neither fear nor anxiety could stop His divine plan.

As I gazed at the audience at the Coretta Scott King Awards Breakfast, I told them, "The Lord doesn't see us the way we see ourselves. I thank God for having a greater plan for me than I could ever have had for myself."

 **SHARON FLAKE** is director of publications at the University of Pittsburgh's Katz Graduate School of Business. The single parent of a teenage daughter, she is a member of Rodman Street Missionary Baptist Church in Pittsburgh. In 1998, Hyperion Press published Flake's first novel, *The Skin I'm In*. Since then she has received national recognition for the book. Flake's second novel, *Money Hungry*, was published in June 2001.

GOD SHOWED UP

Julien Oglesby

Written by Linda Watkins

When I was thirteen, I lived a double life. I went to church every Sunday and was a good student at a Christian school. But after school and on weekends, I drank and did drugs. I was what some call a backsliding Christian.

During seventh grade, I lost interest in school because most of the folks I looked up to didn't see it as a priority. My best friend Darryl was 16 and had dropped out of school. Another good friend, Rehema, was also a high school dropout.[1] Most of my friends were much older than me and hustling in the streets. The more I hung around them, the more attractive their lifestyle seemed.

By that time, I was smoking up to nine cigarettes and three blunts (marijuana sticks) a day. I drank rum and other kinds of hard liquor, sometimes getting drunk. Because my mom was at work all day, she had no idea what I was into. Here she was a schoolteacher and a good Christian woman and I, her only son, was a young, rebellious teenager. My parents are divorced, so my dad wasn't around to discipline me.

More and more, I started staying home from school, pretending to be sick. I would tell my mom I had a migraine headache. Sometimes I did, but often I didn't. She'd let me stay home and after she left for work I'd sleep until noon, then walk around the block. Some days, I'd hang out with friends or stay in and watch TV. That's what I did one particular day that fall.

I woke up that morning thinking, *Uhhhh, I'm not going to school today. It's Friday.* I told my mom I had a migraine headache and felt too bad to go to school. I slept that whole morning and turned on a talk show in the afternoon. After the show, I went to the barber shop for a haircut since I planned to hang out that night. When I got home, I ate dinner and cooled out some more.

Around 8:00 P.M., Darryl and Rehema came by and we wandered toward this one park. It was the hang out spot for couples and folks who did drugs. It was a big park, about the size of a football field, with trees surrounding an open area. The park had a basketball court, tennis court, playground and swings. For two hours, we were shooting the breeze and smoking blunts. It was a beautiful night, the air was kind of crisp and leaves had started falling off the trees.

When me and my friends got bored, we left the park, cut through a path, hopped a couple of fences, and ended up at the back of some stores. We walked around them, crossed the street, and sat on the steps of a nearby apartment building. It wasn't like we knew anyone who lived there. We were just hanging out. Because we were high, none of us were saying much. We were just sitting down watching cars go by on Palisades Avenue, the main street in town. I was hoping someone we knew would pick us up and drive us to New York to hang out or do something. I knew I looked good in my new Timberland boots, jeans, and brand new cream shirt that looked like a jacket.

Everything was cool until all of a sudden I got this feeling that I shouldn't be there. "Go home," something said to me. I started getting chills and feeling sick to my stomach. "Bolt!" the voice said. That's when I started feeling real anxious.

"I think I should go home, get outta here," I told my friends.

"Here you go," Darryl said. He was used to me wanting to go home. A lot of times I'd be bored and decide to leave.

But this time, I really felt strange. Still after several seconds, I decided to stick around and not listen to the voice. I kicked back and relaxed on the step, while my friends headed to a store across the street.

Minutes later, I looked up and fifteen guys were walking down the avenue. They weren't just walking down the street, they were headed toward me! I knew I was in trouble 'cause these guys were much older than me. Several had bad reputations and most of them looked drunk. To them, I probably was a perfect target because I'd just started hanging out so none of them knew me. Plus, I was dressed in clothes that looked new. There I was, alone like a sitting duck.

I knew I should've left. I knew I should've gone home, flashed through my mind over and over. The feelings were even more intense, and I was too scared to think of what might happen next.

Darryl and Rehema had left the store and checked out the scene. They bolted across the street to try to help me. Darryl knew some of the guys but that didn't stop them from messing with me.

"Man, you look real fresh. You just come from the barber shop?" one said. All of them laughed.

"Your mom just take you shoppin'?" another asked. Then he turned to Darryl. "You got some money on you, man?"

"No, I don't have any money. I'm broke, man."

Then he looked at me. Before he could even ask, I said, "No, I don't have money."

"He's got money. He's got money," one of them said. "And yeah, I heard you were talkin' about me."

I don't even know you, I was thinking.

"Hit him! Hit him!" The other guys started shouting.

I backed up two steps, wondering if he was gonna hit me and how bad it would feel. The guy got right in my face—six feet tall, around twenty years old. He was drunk and angry. He tightened his hand into a fist. At that moment I knew there was nothing I could do. Darryl was at the bottom of the stairs and couldn't fight off fifteen guys. Some of them were grabbing Rehema and threatening to attack her. At that point, I knew the *only* One who could help was God. I learned that at church and had prayed since I was a child. So I put my head down and started praying.

"God, I don't know what they want from me. I hope that I get home safely. I should've listened to that voice in my head. But I don't deserve this. I know You can get me outta this. Please help me!"

I looked up at his face and he seemed in shock. He stepped back, just staring at my face and got real quiet. Before, he looked angry, now totally confused. Right then, my cousin Pedro came zooming around the corner on a bike.

Now everybody knew Pedro. He was one of the toughest guys in the neighborhood. Back then, he was twenty-three years old, 6-feet-2, muscular and part of a gang. Pedro was top dog. He was known for fighting, selling drugs, you name it.

My cousin jumped off his bike, looked at me, then looked at all the guys around me.

"What are you all doing?" Pedro asked. All the guys backed off. They were scared. Everybody was scared of him.

Pedro pulled me to the side and asked real smooth, "Are these guys botherin' you?"

Everybody was quiet.

"Julien, I said are they botherin' you?"

"No. Everything's straight," I said, so I wouldn't be a snitch.

Now that really shocked those guys. They thought I'd try to get revenge.

"This is my little cousin," Pedro said, putting his hand on my shoulder. "I don't want no problems. You look after him."

One guy said to me, "If you're related to Pedro, you're our family too now."

Just like that, four of the guys apologized. The others shook my hand. Since that day, I've never had a problem with any of them.

You talk about relieved! God answered my prayer. He also taught me several lessons. One is when you think all hope is lost, put your faith in God because He's right there watching. He actually hears our prayers and wants to answer them. As soon as I prayed, God showed up. He stopped a guy from hitting me and sent my cousin to protect me. If I hadn't prayed, I know I would have wound up in a hospital.

Another lesson is even when we're living a sinful life and don't deserve help, God has mercy on us. He'll come to our rescue if we call Him. God can take our circumstances and turn them around in an instant. That's how much power He has. In Psalm 110:1, the Lord says, "Sit at My right hand, Till I make your enemies your footstool" (NKJV).

Finally, we need to listen when God warns us. When you feel something in your gut, act on it. Now I know that knot in my stomach was nothing but God warning me, telling me to leave what He knew would be a bad situation. If I had listened, I could have avoided the whole situation.

This incident was like a rude awakening for me. It showed me just how much God is right there for us. But it still took years and lots of people's prayers for me to stop doing the things I knew were wrong. Not until I fathered a baby girl out of wedlock did I finally grow up and change my ways. I realized I owed more to God, my family, *and* myself.

Teenagers need to know that momentary pleasures we get from drinking and doing drugs can ultimately cost us our lives, not to mention give us short attention spans and leave us broke. I'm grateful to God for standing by me and helping me through difficult times. As a single father who's blessed with lots of help from my mom and grandmother, I'm determined not to be a deadbeat dad. I want to raise my daughter right and believe I can with God at my side.

 **JULIEN OGLESBY** is a junior at Fairleigh Dickinson University in Teaneck, New Jersey. The psychology major is a member of New Life Covenant Church in Teaneck. During his free time, he enjoys raising his daughter.

---

1. Real names are changed in this story to protect the privacy of Julien's friends and family.

CONCLUSION

You are invited to encounter God, the same God you've read about in this book. He is the God of hope and the God who makes a way out of no way. He is the God who heals and guides our path. He is the God of second chances and the God who sticks closer than a brother.

Almighty God appears to whom He chooses. There are no secret formulas to encountering Him. But the stories in this book illustrate that more often than not God shows up to certain folk. They are the people who seek Him, turn away from sin and follow God.

To seek God is to invite Him to come into your life to help you deal with your problems. Dr. Ben Carson knew that the only way he could pass his chemistry final exam was with God's help. So he prayed for assistance and the Lord gave him a dream. Curtis Martin believed that the only One who could save him from a violent death was Jesus on the cross. So he put his trust in Jesus and, in return, received a second chance at life.

Sometimes our plea for God's intervention is a heartfelt cry for help. "Jesus! Jesus! Jesus!" Evelyn Stokes cried after hearing her son was dead. "Jesus, Jesus, Jesus, Jesus," George Russell pleaded as he lay on a boulevard after his motorcycle accident. In both cases, God heard their cries and met each one at their point of need. Jesus tells us in John 14:6 that no one comes to the Father except through Him.

After seeking God, He calls us to turn away from our sins. Some of us may lie, cheat, curse or provoke fights. Others may be prideful, judgmental, or rebellious. Whatever our sins are — and all of us have at least a few—God asks us to tell Him about them, then change our ways. Dr. Mary Reed finally decided to accept her call to ministry after months of running from God. Gary Shields determined in his heart that he would stop hustling and, instead, pursue the promises of God.

Once we make the decision to turn away from sin, God gives us a fresh start at life. Lewis Lee's favorite Bible verse, 2 Corinthians 5:17, reminds us that if anyone gives his life to Christ, he or she is a new creation. The old things they did are history. All things from then on are new.

But the temptation to fall back into our old habits is still very real. So we also need to follow God. It's not enough to just encounter Him. Consider Chloe Coney. She saw herself as a "good" Christian. She was active in church and blessed with material things. But then God asked her to move beyond her comfort zone to *really* follow Him. God asks us to trust Him more than anyone else in the world and allow Him to guide our lives. By following God's commands, Lamont Couch experienced a miracle —securing all the money needed for his college tuition and debts.

The stories in *God Just Showed Up* tell us that when we look for God, strive to do what's right and follow Him, He shows up. Regardless of when, He's always on time.

There is also another way to encounter God. Once we welcome Jesus Christ—the Son of God—into our hearts, His Spirit lives inside of us. Instead of meeting God in a life-transforming moment, we can experience Him minute by minute, day by day. We can walk and talk with God, just like Adam and Eve in the beginning.

Jesus Christ came to earth. He grew up as a human being. He experienced a painful death on the cross. Then He rose from the dead and returned to His Father in heaven. All of this He did so we could be filled with the presence of God. There in His presence, with His presence in us, we find peace, hope, healing, and direction for our lives.

God is stretching His hand toward each of us, urging us to encounter Him. If you would like to welcome God into your heart, say this simple prayer aloud: *Dear Jesus, I know that I'm a sinner and need Your forgiveness. I believe that You died for my sins. I want to turn away from them and follow You. Please take control of my life and be my Lord and Savior. Amen.*

Brother, Sister, God just showed up.

Other Lift Every Voice Titles

Flame
A Heated Romance Without Him Burns
Vigorously Out of Control

After praying that God would introduce her to a guy, Bacall meets Rory Kerry at a party. He is the student body president, the lead singer in a group called Rise, and to Bacall—perfect. Before completing her last quarter of school, her father offers her the position of Vice President of his record company and she soon realizes that the surprises and changes in her life are just beginning.

ISBN#0-8024-4197-1, Paperback

Planting Seeds of Hope
How to Reach a New Generation of
African Americans with the Gospel

African American Youth are looking for role models they can trust. The network of support is already in place. This book is written to help youth workers, pastors, parents, and others who care about reaching young people with the hope of the Gospel. Written by many who are personally involved with youth, this book explores how to prepare young people for college, counsel African American students in crisis, and balance spirituality and social justice to name a few.

ISBN: 0-8024-5428-3, Paperback

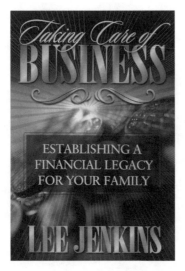

Taking Care of Business
Establishing a Financial Legacy
for Your Family

Most people wrongly believe that the money they earn belongs to them, and they have a right to do with it whatever they please. However, the Biblical view of stewardship involves both ownership and accountability. Lee Jenkins guides us in setting goals in the areas of family, faith, friends, finance and fitness. In addition to providing guidance and direction, he reviews goals that make us think strategically.

ISBN#0-8024-4016-9, Paperback

Sheep In Wolves Clothing
When the Actions of a Christian
Turn Criminal

Jesus warned His followers to beware of "wolves in sheep's clothing." But just as there are wolves in sheep's clothing, there are also "sheep in wolves' clothing": believers in Christ who distance themselves from their faith and walk in the ways of the world. Sheep disguised as wolves can be found almost anywhere. This powerful book is for those beloved sheep who mistakenly believe they no longer belong to the The Good Shepherd.

ISBN #0-8024-6594-3, Paperback